Migrant Mothers in the Digital Age

This book explores the experiences of migrant mothers through the lens of the online communities they have created and participate in. Examining the ways in which migrant mothers build relationships with each other through these online communities and find ways to make a place for themselves and their families in a new country, it highlights the often overlooked labour that goes into sustaining these groups and facilitating these new relationships and spaces of trust. Through the concept of 'digital community mothering,' the author draws links to Black feminist scholarship that has shed light on the kinds of mothering that exist beyond the mother–child dyad. Providing new insights into the experiences of women who mother 'away from home' in this contemporary digital age, this volume explores the concepts of imagined maternal communities, personal maternal narratives, and migrant maternal imaginaries, highlighting the ways in which migrant mothers imagine themselves within local, national, and diasporic maternal communities. As such, it will appeal to scholars and students with interests in migration and diaspora studies, contemporary motherhood and the sociology of the family, and modern forms of online sociality.

Leah Williams Veazey is a Postdoctoral Researcher in the Department of Sociology and Social Policy at the University of Sydney, Australia.

Studies in Migration and Diaspora

Series Editor:
Anne J. Kershen, Queen Mary University of London, UK

Studies in Migration and Diaspora is a series designed to showcase the inter-disciplinary and multidisciplinary nature of research in this important field. Volumes in the series cover local, national and global issues and engage with both historical and contemporary events. The books will appeal to scholars, students and all those engaged in the study of migration and diaspora. Amongst the topics covered are minority ethnic relations, transnational movements and the cultural, social and political implications of moving from 'over there', to 'over here'.

Migration, Education and Translation
Cross-Disciplinary Perspectives on Human Mobility and Cultural Encounters in Education Settings
Edited by Vivienne Anderson and Henry Johnson

Mobile Citizenship
Spatial Privilege and the Transnational Lifestyles of Senior Citizens
Margit Fauser

Nordic Whiteness and Migration to the USA
A Historical Exploration of Identity
Edited by Jana Sverdljuk, Terje Mikael Hasle Joranger, Erika K. Jackson and Peter Kivisto

Higher Education and Social Mobility in France
Challenges and Possibilities among Descendants of North African Immigrants
Shirin Shahrokni

Migrant Mothers in the Digital Age
Emotion and Belonging in Migrant Maternal Online Communities
Leah Williams Veazey

For more information about this series, please visit: https://www.routledge.com/sociology/series/ASHSER1049

Migrant Mothers in the Digital Age

Emotion and Belonging in Migrant Maternal Online Communities

Leah Williams Veazey

Routledge
Taylor & Francis Group

LONDON AND NEW YORK

First published 2021
by Routledge
2 Park Square, Milton Park, Abingdon, Oxon OX14 4RN

and by Routledge
605 Third Avenue, New York, NY 10158

Routledge is an imprint of the Taylor & Francis Group, an informa business

© 2021 Leah Williams Veazey

British Library Cataloguing-in-Publication Data
A catalogue record for this book is available from the British Library

Library of Congress Cataloging-in-Publication Data
Names: Williams Veazey, Leah, 1979- author.
Title: Migrant mothers in the digital age : emotion and belonging in
migrant maternal online communities / Leah Williams Veazey.
Description: Abingdon, Oxon ; New York, NY : Routledge, 2021. |
Series: Studies in migration and diaspora | Includes bibliographical
references and index.
Identifiers: LCCN 2020049909 (print) | LCCN 2020049910 (ebook) |
ISBN 9780367897437 (hardback) | ISBN 9781003020790 (ebook)
Subjects: LCSH: Immigrant women--Social networks--Australia. |
Mothers--Social networks--Australia. | Online social networks--Australia. |
Internet and immigrants--Australia. | Immigrants--Cultural
assimilation--Australia.
Classification: LCC JV9184 .V43 2021 (print) | LCC JV9184 (ebook) |
DDC 305.48/410994--dc23
LC record available at https://lccn.loc.gov/2020049909
LC ebook record available at https://lccn.loc.gov/2020049910

ISBN: 978-0-367-89743-7 (hbk)
ISBN: 978-0-367-76405-0 (pbk)
ISBN: 978-1-003-02079-0 (ebk)

Typeset in Times New Roman
by Taylor & Francis Books

For Greg, Rafael, and Ari

Contents

List of tables   viii
Preface   ix
Acknowledgements   xi
Series editor's preface   xii

1   Introduction   1

2   Migrant maternal online communities   27

3   Migrant mothers' relational, affective, and social settlement
    practices   50

4   Digital community mothering: Gendered digital labour and
    meta-maternal practices   77

5   Connected maternal migrants and imagined maternal
    communities   104

6   Concluding reflections   127

    Appendix 1: The participants   133
    Appendix 2: Interview guide   135
    Index   138

Tables

1.1 Countries of origin of interviewees in Australian migration
     statistics (2019)   3
A.1 Overview of the migrant maternal online communities included
     in the research   133

Preface

This book is deeply entangled in core areas of my life, from my educational background in migration research and personal experiences of migrant motherhood, to my experience in online community management in both professional and voluntary capacities. Born and raised in London, with an Australian mother and British father, I have had dual British-Australian citizenship since birth. I had never lived in Australia, however, until I migrated to Sydney with my British husband and our then two-year-old and three-month-old sons. I had been in Sydney for just over a year when I commenced my research, partly motivated by an interest in how other mothers had experienced and responded to those two upheavals: migration and motherhood.

I am also the daughter of a migrant mother. My mother migrated from Sydney to London in the early 1970s, remaining there for four decades after meeting my father. They raised two children, me and my brother, who as adults live in Sydney and Cape Town respectively, now raising our own young families 'away from home.' Growing up, I remember my mother exchanging fortnightly letters with her parents. I remember stories of my grandmother flying for the first time in her life so she could attend my parents' wedding, the annual crackly phone call on Christmas Day, arguments about politics conducted across the lightweight blue airmail paper, and the worries about health and relationships as my mother's parents aged and eventually died. When we announced our decision to migrate, my mother took it hard, at least partly, I think, because she understood the emotional impact of such a move.

In some ways, my mother's experiences and challenges have been similar to my own, but in other respects, those four decades have changed everything. The weekly airletters were replaced by a family WhatsApp group, pinging messages, photos, jokes and videos between London, Cape Town and Sydney multiple times a day. The crackly Christmas Day phone call transformed into weekly FaceTime video calls during which my children shared songs, news and bedtime stories with their grandparents, aunts, uncles, and cousins. Nevertheless, the distance and time zones created barriers to the sensory intimacies of daily life, and three years after we arrived in Sydney my parents joined us there.

Talking to acquaintances, and participants who migrated before these technologies became commonplace, confirms that while they have transformed some elements of migrant motherhood, others remain familiar. A family friend, who migrated from Switzerland to Sydney in the 1980s, remembers how, shortly after her daughter was born, a nurse put her in touch with another new Swiss mother, sparking a close and long-lasting friendship. The lasting connections that can spring from an encounter with another person from the same country, experiencing migrant motherhood in the same country, clearly precede the advent of Facebook groups. Curiosity about these migrant maternal connections has driven this research.

The months of writing and re-writing this manuscript have coincided with the first months of the global COVID-19 pandemic. On the return journey from a visit to see family and friends in London, we had our first taste of pandemic-related anxiety and restriction when a fellow guest in our Singapore hotel was diagnosed with "novel coronavirus." Overnight, a note was pushed under all guests' doors, and at breakfast the next morning all staff appeared in masks, and guests' temperatures were taken and recorded on entering the dining room. At the time of writing, we are (temporarily? indefinitely?) separated from friends and family overseas by Australia's travel restrictions, including from my paternal grandfather, whose 100th birthday we had celebrated while in London.

During these months, migrant mothers' Facebook groups have been abuzz with the practical and emotional consequences of pandemic-related travel restrictions. Pregnant women wondered whether their own mothers would be able to travel to Australia to support them in childbirth and care for them post-natally; women with sick and vulnerable family members overseas worried about their inability to provide care in person; others reported their efforts to obtain permission to travel to see dying relatives or attend funerals. Overall, migrant mothers appear to be struggling with the sudden undermining of the implicit 'deal' they made with themselves about relocating to Australia – that they and/or their family members would be able to travel to offer care and support in times of need. While these observations are beyond the scope of the research project presented in the following manuscript, they highlight the importance of migrant mothers' online groups as outlets for sharing information and emotions in turbulent times and, more broadly, the significance of care between mothers in the context of migration.

Acknowledgements

I am grateful to Catriona Elder and Susan Goodwin for their support and guidance during the research project on which this book is based, and to Raelene Wilding for her generous mentorship via The Australian Sociological Association's Families & Relationships Thematic Group.

Anne Kershen was an inspiration to me when I studied migration as a master's student in London nearly two decades ago, and I am grateful both for the rigorous grounding her course provided and for her mentorship in stewarding this book to completion all these years later.

Parts of this book have been previously published in articles and book chapters, and I am grateful to the publishers of the following works for their permission to reproduce and reuse them in this book:

Williams Veazey, L. (2019). Glocalised motherhood: Sociality and affect in migrant mothers' online communities. *Feminist Encounters: A Journal of Critical Studies in Culture and Politics, 3(1–2)*, 1–15. doi: https://doi.org/10.20897/femenc/5915.

Williams Veazey, L. (2019). All in the same boat? Migration and motherhood online. In C. Zufferey, & F. Buchanan (Eds.), *Intersections of mothering: Feminist accounts.* Routledge.

Williams Veazey, L. (2020). Migrant mothers and the ambivalence of co-ethnicity in online communities. *Journal of Ethnic and Migration Studies*, 1–17. doi: 10.1080/1369183X.2020.1782180.

Last but not least, I must thank the women who shared their stories and experiences of motherhood and migration with me. Without your generosity of time and spirit, your openness and trust in me, there would be no research project and no book. Truly, this book is for you.

Series editor's preface

People have been migrating since biblical times, propelled by the need for economic advancement, to escape persecution, or both. Until the latter years of the 20th century, recorded patterns of migration and their impact on immigrants and the receiving society were to be found in general historical or sociological texts. From the 1970s onwards, as the migrant presence in the First World became a topic of specific interest and concern, migration began to emerge as a separate subject; though notably up to the time of writing it has yet to be recognised as an independent academic discipline.

Immigrants became categorised as good migrants, those who brought benefits to the society in which they had settled, or bad migrants, those perceived as taking advantage of society and social benefits and contributing little in return. Over recent decades, the categories have grown exponentially and now include asylum seekers, illegal migrants, refugees, and overstayers – those with leave to remain and those on short-term visas. Initially, research tended to focus on male migrants, but more recently female migrants have been placed under the microscope; both genders falling into one or other, or a multiple, of the foregoing categories. Even so, as the author of this volume so perceptively points out, there remained a lacuna in the chronicling – that of migrant mothers.

As a migrant mother herself, the author, Leah Williams Veazey, has explored in depth the experiences of migrant women in Australia who have given birth to, and/or brought up, their children in a country which was not that of their birth: one which for some, even though welcoming, had different practices and traditions in the ways of childbearing. Some of the women she met had arrived in Australia as temporary migrants; as nannies, students, or skilled workers – middling migrants as they are known – then, having married or partnered an Australian, the temporary became permanent. Others had arrived with husbands/partners and found themselves making a new life in a new country and, in some cases, familiarising with a new language.

In the pre-Information Technology age, discovering and researching the lives and survival strategies of these mothering women would have been a challenging task. However, the growth of social media and digital culture enabled the author to contact other migrant mothers over a large area and subsequently record the ways in which 'Facebook' had become a literal – and virtual – life saver. The creation of mothering groups, predominantly from a common national background, provided the women with support, advice, friendship and, in some cases, an administrative role.

In compiling this volume, the author combines a theoretical base together with recent literature on the uses of social media and then draws on the interviews she carried out with 41 mothers from ten countries, covering a geographic spread across Europe, Asia and South America. The result is a fascinating and enlightening insight into the emotional and, at times, traumatic experiences of first-generation migrant mothers in Australia. The book highlights the comparative and contrasting ways in which women from different ethnic backgrounds and traditions develop strategies which enable them to face the demands of motherhood and marriage in an unfamiliar environment. Moving from the personal to the general, Williams Veazey's account additionally provides an insight into the changing face of recent immigrant settlement in Australia, highlighting the fact that migrant groups from Brazil, Nepal, Pakistan, and India, though currently small, are rapidly expanding.

While setting out to focus on community-building by migrant mothers with others from their original home country in the virtual world, the author soon discovered that the virtual frequently led to actual meetings and material activities. However, parallel to these new relationships, transnational mothering was also a feature, as 'grandmothers' introduced their experience of mother-hood to their 'absent' daughters. And whilst some new mothers clung to the traditions of 'home,' others eschewed the 'old ways' and replaced them with new. In this context, Williams Veazey has explored the intersectionality the women under examination have employed in order to coalesce their old lived experiences and traditions with their new lives and the ways they combine imagination with reality and *imagined communities* with the actual.

It is important to stress that this book must not be reserved simply for those concerned with the singular experiences of immigration or motherhood. It is a book which embraces theories which cover the spectrum of media, migration, community, and transnationalism, and then imposes them on real lives, lives lived through social media, and the emotional and stressful demands of the 'real' everyday world of motherhood, children, and marriage. And it is the reaction of husbands and partners to their womenfolk's engagement with the Facebook mothering groups which provides an additional facet to this highly contemporary study. While some of the men supported the women's involve-ment – if not participating themselves – others appeared disinterested or viewed it as encroachment which made excessive demands on their female partners and a waste of their time. These responses tell the reader as much about the different aspects of the male/female partnership as of the role of social media in the modern world.

This is a book which provides a new and impressively researched insight into the migration story, one which though focusing on the digital culture of 2021 at the same time resonates with the experiences of migrant mothers in centuries past. *Migrant Mothers in the Digital Age* deserves a place on the list of all those engaged in researching and understanding the role and experiences of motherhood and the processes of settlement in the female migrant experience.

Anne J. Kershen
Queen Mary University of London
Winter 2020

1 Introduction

Introduction

This book tells the story of how migrant mothers in Australia are making use of new digital platforms to build relationships with each other, to make a place for themselves and their families in a new country, and to navigate their own changing identities as mothers and migrants. Drawing primarily on interviews conducted with 41 migrant mothers from 10 countries, all of whom participate in Facebook groups for migrant mothers in Australia, the book pays particular attention to the administrators of the groups – the women who create and manage the groups – to highlight the labour that sustains the groups and facilitates these new relationships and spaces of trust for their peers. Weaving the stories of the individual migrant mothers, and the stories of the groups as they are created, and as they change and grow, with theoretical concepts drawn from migration, motherhood, and digital studies, this book provides new insights into the experiences of women who mother 'away from home' in this contemporary digital age.

In the months after my own arrival in Australia in 2013, as I sought to orient myself in my new environment as a migrant and mother of two young children, I observed migrant and non-migrant mothers creating and using Facebook groups and other online platforms to connect with other mothers in their local communities. Digging into the literature on migrant motherhood and digital diasporas, I found that the figure of the 'connected maternal migrant' had been largely contained within a transnational carework perspective, focusing on women's connections to children, husbands, and parents from whom they have become separated by migration (e.g. Ahn 2017; Francisco-Menchavez 2018; Madianou 2012; Meyers & Rugunanan 2020; Peng & Wong 2013). In Australia, which has historically accepted family migration, most migrant mothers are co-located with their children, and therefore research based around technology as a means to manage familial separation provides only limited insight into their experiences. At a time when the Australian Census figures make headline news, reporting that "nearly half" of people in Australia are born overseas or have at least one parent born abroad (Australian Bureau of Statistics (ABS) 2016; Hunt 2017), and noting that the overseas-born population is now predominantly

Asian-born rather than European-born, it seems timely to present a book exploring the experiences of first-generation migrants in contemporary Australia and bringing together the experiences of Asian, European, and South American migrants in a single study.

Migration in Australia

As a settler-colonial country, Australia's migration policies have, until recently, been based on the permanent settlement of migrant families. Despite the increase in temporary residence visas since the mid-1990s (J. Collins 2017; Hugo 2006), levels of family migration have remained relatively stable (ABS 2020), and Australia still offers pathways to permanent settlement and citizenship for many immigrants,[1] enabling them to migrate with their partner and children, or to form families post-migration. Australia's historic and continued acceptance of family migration presents a contrasting context to that of many of the studies of transnational mothering, in which regulations, living conditions, or employment exigencies often preclude family migration.

The women who were interviewed for this study came from ten countries across Europe, Asia and South America. They came from India (9), Germany (9), the United Kingdom (8), Sweden (4), Malaysia (3), Ireland (3), Brazil (2), Iran (1), Colombia (1), and Singapore (1). Their countries of origin represent different strands of Australia's migration history. While migrants from Britain and Ireland have had a dominant presence in Australia since its colonisation, and remain the largest group of overseas-born people, the number of migrants from India and Malaysia, for example, remained small until the late 1960s, following the end of the race-based immigration restrictions known as the White Australia Policy. The number of Australian residents born in India quadrupled between 1996 and 2011 (Singh 2016), and Indian-born migrants now make up the third largest group of overseas-born residents after England and China (ABS 2020). Germany has a long and substantial history of migration to Australia, interrupted only by the First and Second World Wars. During the 1850s gold rush, German speakers were the largest group arriving from continental Europe, and the only European group to continue migrating to the Australian colonies in large numbers after 1860 (Jupp 2001, p. 38). After the Second World War, numbers of German migrants increased substantially, mostly due to migration agreements and government assistance schemes, but while Germany is still thirteenth on the list of sending countries, the numbers of German-born residents in Australia has been declining, from 126,450 in 2008, to 114,580 in 2018 (ABS 2019). Brazilian-born migrants, while still making up a relatively small proportion of the overseas-born population, are one of the fastest growing migrant groups, alongside Nepal, Pakistan, and India (ABS 2018). When I looked for Facebook groups for migrant mothers in Australia in 2015–2016, the groups for Brazilian mothers had some of the largest memberships of any groups I found, despite Brazilian-born migrants making up only 0.6% of the overseas-born population.

Table 1.1 Countries of origin of interviewees in Australian migration statistics (2019)

Country	Number	Position among overseas born	% of total overseas born	% of popula- tion, Australia
England[2]	991,530	1	13.5	4
India	592,000	3	8.1	2.4
Malaysia	174,000	9	2.4	0.7
Germany	114,580	13	1.6	0.5
Ireland	87,330	20	1.2	0.3
Iran	71,390	26	1	0.3
Singapore	61,660	27	0.8	0.2
Brazil	46,450	36	0.6	0.2
Colombia	29,840	50	0.4	0.1
Sweden	11,660	73	0.2	0.05
Total overseas born	7,343,000	-	-	29.4
Total population	24,992,760	-	-	-

Sources: ABS '3412.0 – Migration, Australia, 2016–17' (2020) and ABS '34120DO005_201718 Migration, Australia, 2017–18 – Estimated resident population, Country of birth – as at 30 June, 1996 to 2018' (2019).

The diversity of the interview participants reflects the diversity of Australia's migrants. Hailing from ten countries, the women arrived in Australia as students, as nannies, as skilled migrants with firm job offers, as partners of skilled migrants and as spouses of Australian citizens. Many, if not most, initially envisaged a temporary stay in Australia, although many now consider Australia their settled 'home'. In line with the increasing focus on skilled, employed, and educated migrants (and their partners) in Australia's managed migration system (Mares 2017, p. 35), the women in this study, along with most migrant mothers in Australia, can be described as "middling migrants" (Conradson & Latham 2005c; Luthra & Platt 2016). Yet mothers have remained largely invisible in "middling migration" research, which has tended to focus on students, working holidaymakers, and young professionals seeking "overseas experience" (Conradson & Latham 2005b) or hoping to "build a global career" (E. L.-E. Ho 2011), perhaps before returning home to raise a family (Conradson & Latham 2005a).

Migrant mothers and online connectivity: Scoping the field

Literature relating to migrant mothers can be divided into two main bodies of scholarship. One focuses on migrant mothers' experiences of pregnancy, birth, and the immediate postnatal period, mostly from a public health, health sociology, or nursing perspective. Studies in this group have highlighted the failure of health services to meet migrant mothers' specific needs (for example,

Benza & Liamputtong 2014; Hoban & Liamputtong 2012; Renzaho & Oldroyd 2014; Yelland et al. 2015). While the women in these studies are co-located with their children, they are often separated from their usual sources of information and support. They face disempowerment in the face of unfamiliar healthcare systems and cultural expectations and experience social isolation at a time when they need additional support (DeSouza 2005; Tobin et al. 2014). Many of the studies refer to the ongoing impact on migrant mothers' mental health and recommend changes to health and social services to better meet their needs.

The other main body of scholarship on migrant mothers explores maternal practices and ideas about 'good motherhood' and traces how these are changed by migration. Studies in this group draw on insights from motherhood studies that emphasise the contextually inflected and socially constructed nature of motherhood (P.H. Collins 2000, pp. 173–199; Goodwin & Huppatz 2010; Thurer 1995) and position mothering as an intentional social practice involving both rationality and emotion (O'Reilly 2009; Ruddick 1980, 1989). Migrant mothers experience a shift in their perceptions and understandings of good motherhood as they move from one national context to another, and they navigate this complex maternal landscape in dynamic and creative ways (C. Ho 2006; Hondagneu-Sotelo & Avila 1997; Liamputtong 2006; Madianou 2012; Manohar 2013a; Manohar & Busse-Cárdenas 2011; Utomo 2014). Themes in this area include changes in gender roles and work patterns, cultural transmission, and "kin work" (Reynolds & Erel 2018), and transnational carework.

Within these studies of migrant maternal practices, two key focus areas can be identified, both of which can be traced back to the ground-breaking work of feminist migration scholars in the 1990s. The first can be termed 'transnational mothering literature' and has explored how mothers who are separated from their children by migration "transform the meanings of motherhood to accommodate these spatial and temporal separations" (Hondagneu-Sotelo & Avila 1997, see also Parreñas 2001 and Fresnoza-Flot 2009). In recent years, transnational mothering literature has explored the ways mothers who are separated from their children by migration make use of emerging communication technologies to fulfil their altered maternal role from afar (Francisco 2015; Francisco-Menchavez 2018; Madianou 2012; Parreñas 2014; Peng & Wong 2013). Meanwhile, the scholarship around the health and wellbeing of migrant mothers who are co-located with their children has paid relatively little attention to the impact of digital technologies. This book connects these two bodies of scholarship, bringing an awareness of the potentially transformative influence of digital technologies to a study of migrant mothers living with their children in two Australian cities.

The second key focus area explores the role of migrant mothers as community-builders in their country of settlement. These studies, too, have their roots in a cluster of studies by feminist migration scholars in the 1990s (e.g. Hondagneu-Sotelo 1994; see Pessar 1999 for an overview) that drew attention to gendered migration processes and practices and the importance of examining migration from a critical perspective of the household and community (Silvey 2004). In 2009, Gedalof urged feminist migration scholars to re-focus attention on the "*re*productive relocating that migration also necessarily entails" (p. 92), as well as the dislocations and separations. This "reproductive relocation" resonates in Manohar's work with Indian Tamil migrants in the United States, which highlights the intersection of mothering and community-building in migration (2013b) and also resonates with the analysis in this book.

In contrast to the transnational mothering literature, which has effectively explored the potentially transformative influence of digital technologies, the digital has been largely absent from studies of migrant mothers' community-building. For example, Valerie Francisco-Menchavez's recent book (2018) explores both transnational family relationships and the peer "communities of care" created among Filipina migrant domestic workers in New York City, but the impact of evolving communication technologies is only considered in relation to the former aspect. While this undoubtedly reflects the lived reality of the women in Francisco-Menchavez's study, for the more "middling" migrant mothers in my study, digital community-building by and for migrant mothers in Australia was a significant part of their lived experiences. This difference reflects differences in migration regimes (as noted above, Australia has broadly encouraged family migration, whereas the United States has often restricted it, as have many European and Middle Eastern countries), in the socio-economic position of the research participants, and also in the research period. Facebook groups in particular have grown in popularity since 2010, following the launch of a redesigned Groups tool in October of that year. Although groups had existed on Facebook before, the redesigned functionality was explicitly designed "to make sharing and communication with small groups of people easier" (Hicks 2010). In 2017, Facebook claimed that more than 100 million people worldwide were members of "meaningful groups" – "groups that quickly become the most important part of someone's experience on Facebook" – and have publicly stated their aim to increase that number to one billion (Jin 2017). Between 2010 and 2017, therefore, the use of Facebook for creating and participating in groups became a much more common activity. The migrant mothers' groups in the study were all created between 2009 and 2015, and mostly between 2012 and 2014. It is, therefore, perhaps not surprising that studies carried out only a few years before my own found less evidence of the significance of online networks for building community between mothers in migrant contexts.[3]

The research presented in this book brings a digital lens to a study of migrant mothers living with their children in two Australian cities – Sydney and Melbourne. I trace migrant mothers' social relations as they move between online and offline interactions, in a context in which online technologies have become integral to and embedded in many people's experiences of motherhood (Arnold & Martin 2016; Das 2019; S. Johnson 2015; Lupton et al. 2016) and migration (Diminescu 2008; Francisco-Menchavez 2018; Leurs & Ponzanesi 2018). I focus on Facebook groups grounded in the members' new locality but emphasise that these groups exist as part of a complex and dynamic social media landscape. Migrant mothers seek out connections with each other in a plethora of Facebook groups, linked blogs, Twitter, Pinterest, Instagram, MeetUp groups, and more (Williams Veazey 2016). They connect to distant family and friends via WhatsApp groups, Facebook, instant messaging, video calling, online shopping and remittances, and many more (Cabalquinto 2020). The women in my research were often members of dozens of Facebook groups linking them to local mothers in their community, mothers and others in their diaspora networks, people with whom they share a hobby or interest, and, again, many more. The groups at the centre of this study form part of the women's personalised social media landscape, in which they can find tailored information and signal their multiple, shifting, or even conflicting attachments through their online identifications. This means that these migrant maternal groups are neither "virtual ghettoes" (Komito & Bates 2012) nor isolated spaces of "bounded solidarity" in response to discrimination as migrants (Portes & Zhou 1992). They are dynamic assemblages of identification, solidarity, and social support.

A focus on migrant mothers in relation to each other is the 'golden thread' that ties this book together. It therefore resonates with the small but growing literature about the maternal friendships and "horizontal caring" relationships that are built between mothers in migrant contexts, such as Francisco-Menchavez's (2018) research on the "communities of care" developed by Filipina migrant domestic workers in New York City, and Rzepnikowska's (2019) work on "motherly conviviality" between Polish migrant mothers in Barcelona and Manchester.[4] These studies mark a departure from the main body of work on migrant mothers, which places them primarily in relation to partners and children. Taking migrant mothers' Facebook groups as a starting point for this study facilitates an emphasis on connections between mothers. This book also takes a temporally open approach to migration and motherhood, suggesting that both experiences remain salient well beyond the limited 'transitional' periods that have received sustained attention in the relevant literatures. Because the groups are used by mothers of infants as well as of teenagers, and by recently arrived and longer-settled migrants, drawing participants from the groups broadens the scope of the study beyond the pregnancy–birth–postnatal period, and the early months of migrant settlement, which are commonly the focus of research studies in these areas. While making for a complex sample, this diversity brings together the experiences of women often analysed separately, or not at all, offering the opportunity for new insights, connections, and contrasts.

Researching migration and motherhood from a matricentric feminist perspective

This book is grounded in feminist standpoint theories, which understand knowledge and knowers to be socially situated, in contrast to positivist notions of universal and abstract knowledge and knowledge-seeking (Harding 2004). Standpoint theorists understand all knowledge to be partial and produced out of specific social and political contexts (Haraway 1988). Achieving the aim of better knowledge means expanding the diversity of standpoints given epistemic credibility and acknowledging the epistemic resources and deficits offered by each standpoint. Placing those diversely generated knowledges in dialogue with each other can illuminate tacit assumptions, omissions, distortions, and common ground, generating more complete knowledge, empathetic under-standing, or political solidarity (P. H. Collins 1994; Haraway 1991; Hawkesworth 2006). This aim – of knowledge-building from diverse standpoints – has driven this project, which has sought to bring into dialogue the experiences of women from diverse backgrounds, and scholarship from diverse fields of social research.

Specifically, this book also draws on matricentric feminist principles, as outlined in Andrea O'Reilly's *Matricentric Feminism: Theory, Activism and Practice* (2016). Matricentric feminism shares with standpoint feminism a similar experience-centred sensibility. It is framed by social constructionist prin-ciples, understanding motherhood to be socially and historically constructed and contingent. A matricentric feminist approach does not seek to reduce the com-plexity of women's lives and identities into a single and simplified category of 'mother,' but rather recognises that motherhood is a central organising element of the lives of women who are mothers, that motherhood is a significant factor in women's continuing inequality, and that motherhood has been underexplored in both feminist and wider social research. Drawing on matricentric feminist theories, on the experiences of the maternal research participants, and on my position as a feminist mother and researcher, this book presents insights into contemporary experiences of migrant motherhood.

Matricentric feminism positions mothering "more as a practice than an identity" (O'Reilly 2016, p. 4), following Ruddick's argument that mothering is an intentional social practice that involves both rationality and emotion (Ruddick 1980). This emphasis on maternal practices has guided the focus of this project, highlighting what migrant mothers do, think, and feel. A focus on maternal practices, or "motherwork" (P. H. Collins 1994), has a number of advantages. Collins uses "motherwork" to "soften" dichotomies between "private and public, family and work, the individual and the col-lective" (p. 47). The terms 'practice' and 'work' thus embed mothering in its social and political context and emphasise the intentionality and labour involved. They honour the work performed by mothers and admit the pos-sibility that those activities could be undertaken by people other than those with the identity 'mother.' For a scholar of migrant motherhood, the ability to analyse women's experiences through the lens of maternal practices facilitates an analysis of how those experiences and practices change across time and place. Distinguishing between identity and practice also clarifies that mothers may sustain a "selfhood outside of and beyond motherhood" (O'Reilly 2016, p. 135). In this book, I have tried to balance a matrifocal perspective – that is, a focus on mothers and mothering – with an attention to the participants' lives beyond their maternal goals. For example, the book explores women's experiences of friendship and homesickness, shaped by motherhood but not determined by it.

Methods: Scoping, survey, and interviews

This book is primarily informed by the interviews with 41 migrant mothers I conducted between February 2016 and January 2017. Preceding those interviews, I carried out a mapping exercise to investigate the scope of the phenomenon of migrant maternal Facebook groups in Australia, and an online survey, which was completed by 426 migrant mothers located in 33 countries. Despite the focus of this book on material generated by the interviews, the mapping and online survey provided a fundamental grounding for both the interviews and resulting insights.

A sustained search from 2015 to 2016 identified over 80 Facebook groups for migrant mothers in Sydney and around 60 in Melbourne. Faith-based online mothers' groups, e.g. 'Jewish Mums and Bubs Melbourne,' did not fall within the remit of my research, as they did not appear to be primarily focused on migration, although some members may be migrant mothers. These figures are certainly an underestimate, even as a snapshot of a rapidly changing phenomenon.[5] For example, when I first searched for groups in 2015, the group for Indian mothers in Sydney featured in this book had not yet been created. Between January 2016, when I first noted its existence, and June 2016, when I interviewed one of the creators of the group, it had already doubled in size to 5,000 members. Since then, the group has grown further and has 'sister' groups in Melbourne, Perth, and Brisbane, as well as a linked group for Indian fathers in Sydney. The scoping exercise provided a sense of the scale and shape of online groups specifically aimed at migrant mothers in Australia and also provided a basis for the recruitment of participants. The administrators of as many of the Sydney- and Melbourne-based groups as possible were approached to disseminate the online survey and to participate in interviews.

Similarly to the scoping exercise, the survey was designed to establish a basis of knowledge about the topic, highlight gaps and assumptions I brought to the research, and as a means of initiating contact with potential research participants. Specifically, the survey aimed to discover what kinds of online resources migrant mothers used as part of their migration and motherhood experiences, particularly relating to their experiences of mothering away from home. The survey was open for one year and was designed to be completed by women living in any country in the world, although it was only available in English, thus limiting its reach. The survey was completed by 426 women, 54% of whom were living in Australia at the time of survey completion, with a further 9% in the UK, and 8% in New Zealand. Over a third of respondents had most recently lived in the UK prior to their migration. Although women living in 33 countries and holding 55 nationalities[6] completed the survey, there is clearly a skew towards women with experience of living in Australia, the UK, and New Zealand, undoubtedly reflecting both the networks through which the survey was disseminated and the English-language context. The survey data should therefore not be viewed as representative of migrant mothers everywhere (to be clear, it was not designed to be so) but rather as complementary to the interviews conducted with women living in Australia.

Over half of survey respondents had joined an online group for mothers specifically from their country of origin or cultural background, and of those, 69% had met up with someone in person who they had initially got to know through the online group. 85% accessed the groups via an internet-enabled phone or smartphone, indicating the importance of this mode of access. 61% saw posts from the group at least once a day, and nearly a third said they saw such posts "multiple times most days."

Survey respondents were asked to name groups and resources which they had found useful in their experiences of migration and motherhood – specifically in their experience of being a mother away from 'home' – and, where appropriate, their answers were included in the mapping exercise and participant recruitment process. Perhaps more significant to the shaping of this book was the way the creation, dissemination, and analysis of the survey developed my understanding of the phenomenon at hand and the context in which it had developed. For example, the survey asked about respondents' reasons for migrating and gave six options[7] plus the invitation to add information under an 'other' category. Over half of the 95 'other' responses gave their spouse as the main reason for moving. This included reasons framed romantically ("to be with the love of my life"), legalistically ("my partner doesn't have a visa for the UK"), and in terms of relationship balance ("Australian husband has been overseas with me for the last 10yrs, time to be close to his family").

This highlighted a common motivation for migration – love and marriage – and more broadly the centrality of relational rather than individual motivations. This relational view of migration became central to the project and subsequently framed much of the analysis, such as the focus on "relational settlement." The survey findings also highlighted the relevance of both "lifestyle migration" (Benson & Osbaldiston 2014) and "love migration" (Djurdjevic & Roca Girona 2016) frameworks, as well as a sensitivity to uneven gender dynamics in migration decision-making (Hiller & McCaig 2007). This was confirmed by the experiences of the interview participants, two-thirds of whom cited either their partner[8] or their partner's work opportunities as their main motivation for migrating.

To give a second example: over a third of survey respondents had become mothers for the first time more than five years after they first migrated. In addition, while the majority of their children were five years old or younger at the time of the survey, nearly 20% of the children were older than five and 4% were older than twelve. As I had initially presumed the study would focus on women for whom matrescence[9] and migration were broadly coterminous and recent, this finding led me to broaden my expectations of potential interview participants and to interrogate the 'new mother, new migrant' perspective with which I had approached the project. What might these migrant maternal groups offer women who had older children, or who had migrated many years prior to embarking on motherhood?

Having mapped the field and identified key themes from the survey data, I embarked on the semi-structured, in-depth interviews which would form the heart of the project. In contrast to some scholars of the digital, who advocate digital methods for digital phenomena (e.g. Kozinets 2015), I settled on mostly in-person interviews for methodological and ethical reasons. I take a feminist digital sociological stance, as outlined by Ferreday (2013), who emphasises that digital technologies "are not simply media texts to which we can apply theoretical tools, they are records of (and in themselves constitute) lived experience" (pp. 55–56). In addition, I wanted to "explore the textures of social life which result as people combine online and offline experiences in complex, and unpredictable fashion" (Hine 2015, p. 13). Interviews allowed me to explore migrant mothers' lived experiences and to incorporate their interpretations of their experiences in my analysis. In their interviews, participants discussed the significance of reading posts in the group, or simply being a member of it, as well as interactions beyond the visible areas of the group, such as private messages between members, text messages to friends inspired by a post on the group, or group conversations happening on a different platform, such as WhatsApp. These insights could not be gained from an analysis of posted content. Focusing only on content that is visible (for example, in content analysis or participant observation) privileges the perspective of the person who writes and posts the content over the perspective of the many others who read it, whether they respond or not (Sun et al. 2014; Yang et al. 2017). Using interview data enabled the use of direct quotes from the participants without jeopardising their anonymity. (Verbatim quotes from online content may be identified using a search function, thereby undermining participants' anonymity.) Moreover, talking to migrant mothers about their experiences, and the meanings they ascribe to those experiences, about their imagined pasts, presents, and futures, is central to the purpose of this research.

Interviews have their own limitations, of course. People's memories do not always tally with the evidence of the site, and participants attribute motivations to other members which may not be reliable. Nevertheless, qualitative interviews align well with the project's research objectives and its ethical stance. Drawing on Nissenbaum's (2011) concept of "contextual integrity," I determined that the norms and structures of the groups indicated a reasonable expectation that members' posted content would be observed only by members of the group. Closed groups are not open to the public. Members must request access and are screened to ensure they fit membership criteria. While anyone can see the group's name and description, only group members can see content posted in the group. In addition, my preliminary research and personal experience of similar groups indicated that these groups are used for support on personal and intimate issues. Some group members may be isolated, vulnerable, and unable to access alternative support. As such, I considered the risk that my presence might inhibit women from seeking support from the group grave enough to exclude methods that required direct observation of the groups. This is also consistent with extant literature noting resistance from online community members to being used in research (Eysenbach & Till 2001; Hudson & Bruckman 2004; Johnson et al. 2018; King 1996).

The 41 interviewees were all mothers, had moved to Australia from another country, and were members of a Facebook group for migrant mothers in Australia (See Appendix 1). Participants were aged between 30 and 49, mostly married (to men), and had been in Australia between six months and 28 years. Fifteen of the participants had an administrator role in the group. All Facebook groups in the study were based around a specific and defined migrant identity, either national (e.g. British), regional (e.g. Scandinavian), or linguistic (e.g. Spanish speaking). Although the study approached the groups as online phenomena, they are examples of an "embedded, embodied and everyday" internet (Hine 2015). All groups facilitated offline encounters as well as online interactions, although not all participants availed themselves of these opportunities.

The interviews were conducted in settings chosen by the interviewee and usually frequented by them as a part of their daily life, such as their work-place, their home, or a café in their local area. In some cases, their children were present for some or all of the interview. Occasionally, a partner or friend was present at the beginning or end of the interview. Within the formal interview framework of consent procedures and so on, the interviews had a conversational style, encouraging informal talk and reciprocity (Roulston 2008). Although the same topics were covered in each interview, usually in a similar order, the conversations were often wide-ranging and sometimes took surprising tangents (see Appendix 2 for interview guide).

Migrant, mother, researcher, community manager: Situating myself in the research

When I conceived this project in mid-2014, hurriedly sketching out the parameters of a potential research proposal in the precious minutes while my youngest child napped, I was the mother of a one-year-old and a three-year-old. We had moved from London to Sydney the previous year as a bit of an experiment, taking advantage of the portability of small children and the relative freedom of being on maternity leave from my job as an online community manager. These experiences, and their intersections with my social locations in terms of gender, race, class, and so on, shaped my approach to the research and my relationship with the research participants and the data we produced together. All the research participants shared personal histories that included migration and motherhood. Most were, like me, middle-class, well-educated, and married to men, and had migrated to Australia for multifactorial reasons including work, study, love, and lifestyle. No participant was more than ten years older or younger than me. We were all 'fluent in Facebook' with easy access to digital technology. As an administrator of Facebook groups myself – although not the specific type of group explored in this research – and former professional community manager, I shared with the administrator-participants an understanding of the tools and tasks involved.

In other areas, however, we were less able to draw on common ground. Ethnicity, nationality, length of time since migration, age of children, mother tongue, and current place of residence, were among the points of difference which constituted different experiences of, and perspectives on, the topics of research. In reflecting on my positionality and its influence on the research, Manohar's (2013c) conceptualisation of shared social locations in research as a dynamic process of strategic presentation, a contextual, performative, and sometimes tenuous process, more than a static status based on common background or experience, was particularly influential. Louise Ryan's (2008) reflections on the emotions of conducting migration research as a migrant researcher and the potential for interviews to become "emotional encounters" which may be uneasy for both researcher and participant (pp. 309–310) also resonated with my own experiences.

As a researcher, I experienced the vulnerability of transparency that resulted from heavily overlapping social locations. For example, I felt that the British women could infer information from my accent and other non-verbal cues about my class and geographical origins in a way that most other interviewees could not. Although I invited this sense of commonality by discussing my own experiences and background, and although this sense of shared identity may have facilitated access to potential participants (for example, the participants from the British and Irish group were much quicker to volunteer), this transparency was unexpectedly uncomfortable. Perhaps it was uncomfortable for the participants as well.

I consciously deployed our shared maternal status to curate the interview as a conversational encounter rather than a hierarchical extraction of experience. In arranging the interviews, I explained that I too had young children and understood the logistics of nap times and school-runs that made scheduling difficult, encouraging participants to choose a time and location to suit their needs. As arrangements also had to suit my own needs, for example, to be back in time to pick up children from preschool, those logistical negotiations became a choreographed performance that highlighted our shared maternal locations. In addition, as a student with young children, I inhabited a kind of liminal social status, side-stepping some of the potential sensitivities around mothers working outside the home or staying at home with children (Douglas & Michaels 2004). On one notable occasion, this strategic performance of shared motherhood failed. Despite my efforts, it became clear during an interview with one of the Indian participants that she had not recognised me as a fellow mother but only as a white, presumably Australian, researcher. Late in the interview, in response to one of my comments about my children, she expressed surprise and visibly relaxed. Our conversation became more friendly and less stilted.

In her article, Manohar (2013c) recalls how some interview topics precipitated a refusal by her interview participants of the shared social location she had tried to deploy for the purposes of building rapport and eliciting research data. When discussing motherhood, marriage, and domestic issues, her participants emphasised that she, a single, childless woman, could not share their perspective. Some participants positioned her as a daughter or younger relative, and in response, she positioned herself as a "learner/researcher" rather than a "peer" when discussing these issues. Like Manohar, I found that the sense of shared social location shifted when discussing certain topics. In the interview with Susie, we established many areas of shared experience, such as growing up in particular areas of London, mothering two children as Londoners living in Sydney, and our shared Jewish heritage. When she raised her worries about her children growing up in a different country to where she had been raised, I shared my experiences of being raised by a migrant mother, and Susie then positioned me in a daughterly role. She thanked me for sharing my experiences and then noted, "It's like I'm looking at [my daughter] in – however old you are …" Although only six years older than me, at this point, Susie identified more with my mother than with me. I deployed my dual location as both a migrant mother and daughter of a migrant mother to bring relevant experiences to the interview and enable an exploration of issues from multiple perspectives. In this way, our shared social locations were contextual and dynamic.

In an interview with one of the British migrants with Indian heritage, I noted these shifting dynamics and the positioning of me as an "insider" at some points and "outsider" at others. When Kavita spoke about her hectic London lifestyle, we positioned ourselves as fellow middle-class Londoners, and when we talked about Skype or ageing parents, we were fellow migrants with family responsibilities overseas. When she greeted me at her door wearing her dressing gown, requesting a couple of minutes to get dressed before starting the interview and laughing "you know what it's like," we were fellow mothers of small children juggling multiple priorities and morning routines. But during discussions of Indian traditions around pregnancy and birth, the importance of passing on Indian culture to her daughter, or the gender and family dynamics she attributed to her ethnicity, Kavita positioned me as an outsider. She felt the need to explain things to me because I did not share the knowledge she possessed as a mother with Indian heritage. As a fellow Londoner of a similar age, she did expect me to be familiar with some elements of Indian culture, such as festivals and foods, whereas the participants who had migrated from India assumed no such shared knowledge in this area. Awareness of our respective social locations facilitated an understanding of where those locations might intersect differently and create a different assemblage of understanding and experience. In these research encounters, sameness and difference, power relations, empathy and identification, are all dynamic and negotiated, affecting the information shared and the emotional temperature of the encounter (Manohar 2013c; Mullings 1999; Rzepnikowska 2019, p. 44; Valentine 2002, p. 122).

The diversity of the participants, and an understanding of identities and social locations as intersectional (Collins & Bilge 2016), meant that a straightforward understanding of myself as either "insider" or "outsider" was impossible to maintain (Dwyer & Buckle 2009). The mapping exercise and online surveys were methodological tools for widening the frame of the research beyond my own experience before plunging into the interpersonal research space of the interviews. During the recruitment, interview, and analysis phases, I reflected in audio and written memos on how my own experiences and social locations may have intersected or contrasted with the participants,' how this may have affected our interactions, and my intuitive or emotional response to the participants' narratives. Field notes also recorded perceived changes in 'emotional pitch' during individual interviews, when discussing specific topics or recalling particular events appeared to increase the emotional intensity of the interview. In reviewing memos from the transcription phase, I found a particularly striking note in which I had described feeling "teary" and "homesick" while reading transcripts, "like I want to pick up my babies and take them to see where we all come from." I also noted that this was highly unusual for me and unrelated to any specific trigger outside the research process. This echoes Ryan's (2008) experience of interviews with fellow migrant mothers as "emotional encounters" which could be overwhelming, unexpected, and uneasy for both researcher and participant (pp. 309–310).

As Doucet (1998) argues, reflecting on how her experience of mothering affected her analysis of interview data, "the ways in which we 'see' and 'hear' the individuals whom we interview will make a difference to how we construct theory from their words, experiences, and lives." Although grounded in the data, as was Doucet's analysis, this project has undoubtedly been shaped by both my personal biography and a feminist thematics that tends to highlight themes of gender, agency, resistance, inequality, freedom, and power.

A matricentric study at the intersections of migration and digital cultures

This book is a sociological investigation of migration, motherhood, and digital cultures, grounded in feminist epistemologies, ontologies, and research principles – specifically standpoint, intersectional, and matricentric feminist perspectives. These perspectives have guided the project from the formulation of the research topic and questions, the exploration of relevant literature, the research design and implementation, to the analysis, representation, and presentation of the findings. Social lives and processes are understood as significantly structured by gender, and motherhood is understood as being experienced and regulated in socially, culturally, and historically specific ways. Within those social structures and regulations, migrant mothers are positioned as active and creative agents, capable of self-initiated projects and of co-constructing interpretations of their experiences (Gatt et al. 2016; Manohar 2013a).

Mothers' lives are worthy of scholarly attention and yet have been sidelined in mainstream social research, including migration research. Investigations of mothers' lives have often been fragmented into splinters of experience, such as experiences of pregnancy, birth, early motherhood, carework, or employment, or have been premised on a white, middle-class, heterosexual norm. In this book, I seek to present diverse and well-rounded examinations of contemporary motherhood. I have balanced a matrifocal perspective – that is, a focus on mothers and mothering – with an attention to women's lives beyond motherhood. In addition, women's identities, positions, and experiences are understood intersectionally as being produced by "multiple social structures and processes" (Anthias 2012, p. 106). Societies and structures of power are also understood intersectionally as "shaped not by a single axis of social division, be it race or gender or class, but by many axes that work together and influence each other" (Collins & Bilge 2016, p. 2). Women's experiences of motherhood are shaped by their experiences of migration and vice versa. Furthermore, their experiences and the way they understand them are shaped by factors such as class, race, ethnicity, and age in ways that "build on each other and work together" (Collins & Bilge 2016, p. 2). Such factors and their intersections are dynamic and unstable, and this becomes even more apparent in a migration context, with its focus on change, movement, and transitions. Throughout the research, I have remained attentive to the specificities of participants' experiences and the commonalities between them, using the principles and tools of relational intersectionality to manage this complexity (Collins & Bilge 2016). Relationality, with its focus on the "fundamental interconnectedness among human beings" (Nedelsky 2011) is described by Collins and Bilge (2016) as one of the "guideposts" for thinking through intersectionality (p. 25), and it has also been a guidepost for this book.

Migration as relational and emotional

This book is a study of migrant motherhood in Australia, viewed through an emotional and relational lens. It is also an exploration of online sociality and how the affordances of social media sites have affected how contemporary migrants find their place in their country of settlement. It explores how migrant mothers position themselves in relation to particular migrant and maternal identities, navigate what it means to be a mother from 'there' raising children 'here,' and engage with personal maternal narratives and socially constituted maternal imaginaries which have been changed by the migrant experience.

Relational sociology and relational settlement

Relational sociology asserts the primacy of interactions, social ties, and networks (Prandini 2015, p. 7). Ontologically speaking, the self is relational because human beings become who they are through their relationships (Nedelsky 2011). Although true for everyone, motherhood is perhaps the relational state *par excellence*. Motherhood as a category bears within it the implicit relationship between mother and child. Conversely and relatedly, all human life begins in relationship to our mother, as "we take shape within the womb of our mother, as a parasite upon her, and we are born helpless and incomplete" (Crossley

2010, p. 3). In migration studies, relational approaches have helped scholars to explore the ways in which personal connections enable and constrain mobility, sometimes referred to in terms of "network capital" (e.g. Wong & Salaff 1998).

Central to this exploration is the concept of "relational settlement." In 2008, Diminescu coined this phrase to describe how migration decisions are facilitated by connections to people in the country of migration (2008, pp. 570–572). Diminescu's focus here could also be described as "relational *mobility*." A relational approach is, however, important not just for explaining (im)mobility but also for exploring "the complexities of inhabitance" (Gedalof 2009, p. 87). Drawing together Diminescu's terminology and Gedalof's focus on the "*repro-ductive relocating that migration also necessarily entails*" (2009, p. 92), I deploy the term "relational settlement" to describe how migrants build a sense of *belonging* through the establishment of *new* social networks and relationships (Williams Veazey 2019, p. 2). Used in this way, "relational settlement" refers to relational practices that have a "home-building" sensibility, aiming to create "affective building blocks" of community, security, familiarity, and possibility (Hage 1997). In this dual usage, we can see the relevance of relationships across distance *and* in proximity; for mobility *and* "inhabitance" (Gedalof 2009; see also Ebaugh & Curry 2000). As Gedalof (2009) argues, a relational approach highlights the importance of "nearness, inter-dependency and the construction of bonds between selves" in a migrant context (p. 93) and brings to light the often overlooked work performed by mothers to achieve stability and belonging for themselves and their family.

Emotional dimensions of migration: Affective settlement

Closely linked but distinguishable from relational settlement is a process I term "affective settlement." On a descriptive level, affective settlement refers to the salience of emotions in the process of migration and, more specifically, in the process of building a sense of home and belonging in a new place. On an analytical level, affective settlement refers to the role of the emotions in facilitating or inhibiting those processes. This book moves between those two registers, describing the experiences of migrant mothers in terms of loneliness and friendship, homesickness and belonging, guilt and love, and also how migrant mothers utilise these shared emotional experiences to build relation-ships of "horizontal care" (Francisco-Menchavez 2018) and a sense of belonging for themselves and their family. One of the key roles of the online communities built by the migrant mothers is to act as a social and emotional safety net, particularly during the precarious periods of new migranthood and/or new motherhood.

In this focus on the emotional aspects of migration and settlement, I draw on recent scholarship on the emotions of migration which seeks to provide a counterbalance to the "dominance of economic and political analyses of migration" (Boccagni & Baldassar 2015). In common with most sociological scholarship in this area, emotions are framed in this book as embodied, social, and relational (Ahmed 2004; Wilding et al. 2020), and thus deeply entangled in social and cultural expectations which are themselves contextual and dynamic. In the context of digital connectivity and migration, it is important to consider "what forms of emotionality new kinds of platform sociality might involve" (Alinejad & Ponzanesi 2020 p. 622). This book seeks to trace the forms of emotionality circulating around the online communities of migrant mothers, investigating both the "emotional affordances" of the online groups (Bareither 2019) and their consequences in the social lives of migrant mothers.

Migrant maternal imaginaries

A third key concept for this book is the migrant maternal imaginary (Williams Veazey 2020).[10] The migrant maternal imaginary can be defined as a framework of identity, based on a mother's understanding of herself as a mother from a specific place or culture and living in a different geographical and cultural space. In navigating her role as a 'good' mother, she draws on ideas about what mothers from her place or culture of origin (should) do, and on ideas about what mothers where she now lives (should) do. Migrant mothers use their migrant maternal imaginary to make decisions about maternal practices, and, more broadly, it frames how they think and feel about their maternal experiences and identity. This definition draws on Kanno and Norton's (2003) reworking of Benedict Anderson's (2006 [1983]) concept of "imagined communities." For Kanno and Norton (2003), imagined communities provide "a theoretical framework for the exploration of creativity, hope, and desire in identity construction" (p. 248). They argue that the community (or communities) people imagine themselves to belong to influences their choices and can (re)frame their interpretation of their action. Imagined communities, they suggest, "expand our range of possible selves" (p. 246).

Lennon's (2015) description of the imaginary as "the way in which we not only think, but also feel our way around" (p. 1) is particularly pertinent to this book, which explores the ways migrant mothers activate and manifest their imaginaries as they "feel [their] way around" new places and roles. Imaginaries are, as Lennon argues, deeply infused with emotion. How the mothers in this study feel about their identities, practices, and the multiple social groupings with which they interact reveals the "emotional contours" (p. 1) of migrant motherhood. As well as being central to identity and emotion, the imagination can also be a decision-making tool or coping mechanism for migrants, as Adams (2004) shows in her study of cross-national couples' discussions about where they should live.

The migrant maternal imaginary is not so much a means by which specific national or ethnic models of motherhood are (re)produced; rather, it is a framework for thinking about the experiential and abstract resources on which mothers draw as they try to make sense of their identity as a mother 'away from home' and try to navigate what it means to be a good mother in this context. Through their memories, imaginaries, and interactions with people and institutions, migrant mothers know that multiple possibilities of good mothering co-exist. In a digital age, online groups are key sites in which these multiple possibilities are displayed and discussed. In contrast to the print media central to Benedict Anderson's concept of nineteenth-century "imagined communities," social media exist in a highly heterogeneous and participative media landscape and have much looser connections to national borders. It is in this context that migrant mothers engage with migrant maternal Facebook groups, alongside other online and offline resources, to assemble a sense of good motherhood that feels authentic and meaningful to them, to observe what other mothers in their (online and offline, migrant and non-migrant) communities are doing, and to foster a sense of belonging as a mother in migration.

Overview of the book

Chapter 2 introduces the migrant maternal Facebook groups, which are this study's research sites. The groups are described and placed in the broader context and history of parents' groups in Australia. Their origin stories are explained in relation to the personal mothering and migration stories of the women who created them, and in the context of the rising popularity of Facebook groups. The chapter outlines the main activities undertaken in the groups, focusing on the exchange of information and the ways in which this exchange is part of a social strategy undertaken by women in an attempt to navigate their lives as migrant mothers in Australia. This chapter also introduces the reader to the migrant mothers who create and participate in these groups.

Chapter 3 explores the emotional, relational, and social dimensions of migrant motherhood. Drawing out the mothers' experiences of isolation, friendship, homesickness, guilt, failure, and disconnection, the chapter explores how these emotions are seen as barriers to feeling 'at home' in Australia. Participating in migrant maternal online communities helps them not necessarily to overcome these emotions but to contextualise them and reconcile them with the possibility of belonging. The chapter explores how the online groups facilitate different modes of sociality, from casual intimacy, through intermediate ties, to heartfelt friendship. These social relations enable migrant mothers to explain and explore their emotions in relation to migration and motherhood. Key concepts of *relational settlement, affective settlement*, and *migrant maternal sociality* are defined and explored.

Chapter 4 focuses on the practices of the migrant mothers who run the groups, and how they shape them into gendered and geographically based sites of belonging and trust. Viewing the work of the groups' administrators as intentional and significant, I introduce the term *meta-maternal practices* to describe how the group administrators establish a behavioural norm of compassion between mothers and build migrant maternal solidarities. Drawing on Black feminist scholarship, I suggest that these meta-maternal practices constitute a form of digital "community mothering" (P.H. Collins 1991, 2000; Edwards 2000), in which a maternal ethic of care extends beyond the needs of one's own children into maternally based community service and community-building. This chapter makes visible the unpaid, gendered labour involved in community-building, expanding on scholarship within the field of gender and migration that positions the work of migrant women as fundamental to their families' settlement experiences (Manohar 2013b; Hondagneu-Sotelo 1994). In highlighting the labour involved in creating and maintaining these online groups, I also draw on feminist scholars of technology who conceptualise online community management and other social media practices as gendered, relational, and emotional labour (De Winter et al. 2017; Jarrett 2016; Portwood-Stacer 2014).

Chapter 5 introduces the concepts of *imagined maternal communities, personal maternal narratives* and *migrant maternal imaginaries*. It highlights how migrant mothers imagine themselves within local, national, and diasporic maternal communities, and within an individual maternal narrative that may have been disrupted by migration. Migrant mothers, even first-time mothers, bring with them knowledge, practice, and values accumulated through their upbringing and observations of maternal practices. These accretions of knowledge, practice, and values form a narrative of themselves as mothers in relation to an imagined national community, which often lies largely unexamined until activated by their move into motherhood. Decision-making around maternal practices brings this narrative into focus, as it is challenged by alternative narratives and lived experiences of motherhood. These challenges are also important moments of identity construction, as women enact or shift their attachments to their imagined communities, reconstructing or reconciling their personal narratives in their changed context. The chapter explores how digital connections in the form of localised migrant maternal online communities provide opportunities for migrant mothers to discuss their decision-making around maternal practices, their observations of local maternal practices, and their attempts to incorporate or resist culturally inflected elements into their mothering.

In the concluding chapter, I summarise the key findings from this research project and outline their significance for scholarship and practice, focusing on ways in which migrant mothers could be better supported.

Notes

1 In 2017–18, around half of all permanent visas were granted to people who were in Australia already on a temporary visa (Department of Home Affairs 2018).
2 In the statistics on overseas-born residents, the Australian Bureau of Statistics separates the constituent nations of the United Kingdom. By contrast, the online groups in this study tended to bring together migrants from not only the United Kingdom but also Ireland.
3 For example, Manohar's 2013 article on community-building by Tamil women migrants in the US does not mention online networks, despite drawing on the experiences of migrants to Atlanta, Georgia, many of whom migrated there specifically for its high-tech industry.

4 See also Gilmartin and Migge (2016) for a discussion of friendships between migrant mothers in Ireland.
5 Factors inhibiting the search include numerous languages used, multiple terms for 'mother' in all languages, differences in geographical focus and terms to describe it, privacy settings of Facebook groups, and the uneven popularity of Facebook amongst migrant populations. The search started in late 2015 and was revisited over the following year. New groups appeared; some grew quickly, others dwindled or appeared inactive.
6 Respondents were able to select more than one nationality. The top three nationalities recorded were British, Australian and US-American.
7 Lifestyle (51%), partner's job or career prospects (50%), experience something different (37%), my job or career prospects (24%), to be closer to family (7%), fleeing war, natural disaster etc. (2%).
8 Including: marriage, settling with partner, love, and partner's desire to return to Australia.
9 Matrescence is a term coined by Dana Raphael (1975) to describe the experience of becoming a mother for the first time.
10 This section is reproduced with permission of the publisher from Williams Veazey, L. (2020). Migrant mothers and the ambivalence of co-ethnicity in online communities, *Journal of Ethnic and Migration Studies*. doi: 10.1080/1369183X.2020.1782180.

References

Adams, J. (2004). The imagination and social life. *Qualitative Sociology*, 27(3), 277–297. doi:10.1023/B:QUAS.0000037619.28845.ef.
Ahmed, S. (2004). Collective feelings: Or, the impressions left by others. *Theory, Culture & Society*, 21(2), 25–42. doi:10.1177/0263276404042133.
Ahn, K. (2017). Ambivalent gender power in interstitial space: The case of transnational South Korean mothers. *Asian Journal of Women's Studies*, 23(2), 139. doi:10.1080/12259276.2017.1317701.
Alinejad, D., & Ponzanesi, S. (2020). Migrancy and digital mediations of emotion. *International Journal of Cultural Studies*, 23(5), 621–638. doi:10.1177/1367877920933649.
Anderson, B. R. O. G. (2006). *Imagined communities: Reflections on the origin and spread of nationalism*. New York; London: Verso (Original work published 1983).
Anthias, F. (2012). Transnational mobilities, migration research and intersectionality. *Nordic Journal of Migration Research*, 2(2), 102–110. doi:10.2478/v10202-011-0032-y.
Arnold, L. B., & Martin, B. A. (Eds.). (2016). *Taking the village online: Mothers, motherhood, and social media*. Bradford, ON: Demeter Press.
ABS (Australian Bureau of Statistics). (2016). 2024.0 – Census of population and housing: Australia revealed [Press release]. Retrieved from http://www.abs.gov.au/ausstats/abs@.nsf/Latestproducts/2024.0Main Features22016.
ABS. (2018). 3412.0 – Migration, Australia, 2016–17. Retrieved from https://www.abs.gov.au/AUSSTATS/abs@.nsf/Lookup/3412.0Main+Features32016–32017?OpenDocument.
ABS. (2019). 34120DO005_201718 Migration, Australia, 2017–18. Estimated resident population, Country of birth – as at 30 June, 1996 to 2018. Retrieved from https://www.abs.gov.au/AUSSTATS/abs@.nsf/DetailsPage/3412.02017–02018?OpenDocument.
ABS. (2020). 3412.0 – Migration, Australia, 2018–19. Retrieved from https://www.abs.gov.au/ausstats/abs@.nsf/Latestproducts/3412.0Main%20Features32018–32019?opendocument&tabname=Summary&prodno=3412.0&issue=2018–2019&num=&view=.

Bareither, C. (2019). Doing emotion through digital media: An ethnographic perspective on media practices and emotional affordances. *Ethnologia Europaea*, 49(1). doi:10.16995/ee.822.

Benson, M., & Osbaldiston, N. (2014). *Understanding lifestyle migration: Theoretical approaches to migration and the quest for a better way of life.* London: Palgrave Macmillan.

Benza, S., & Liamputtong, P. (2014). Pregnancy, childbirth and motherhood: A meta-synthesis of the lived experiences of immigrant women. *Midwifery*, 30, 575–584. doi:10.1016/j.midw.2014.03.005.

Boccagni, P., & Baldassar, L. (2015). Emotions on the move: Mapping the emergent field of emotion and migration. *Emotion, Space and Society*, 16, 73–80. doi:10.1016/j.emospa.2015.06.009.

Cabalquinto, E. C. (2020). Elastic carework: The cost and contradictions of mobile caregiving in a transnational household. *Continuum*, 34(1), 133–145. doi:10.1080/10304312.2019.1703903.

Collins, J. (2017). Australia's new guest workers: Opportunity or exploitation? In M. Boese, & V. Marotta (Eds.). *Critical reflections on migration, 'race' and multiculturalism.* London: Routledge.

Collins, P. H. (1991). The meaning of motherhood in Black culture and Black mother-daughter relationships. In P. Bell-Scott (Ed.), *Double stitch: Black women write about mothers & daughters.* Boston: Beacon Press.

Collins, P. H. (1994). Shifting the center: Race, class, and feminist theorizing about motherhood. In E. N. Glenn, G. Chang, & L. R. Forcey (Eds.), *Mothering: Ideology, experience, and agency.* New York; London: Routledge.

Collins, P. H. (2000). *Black feminist thought: Knowledge, consciousness, and the politics of empowerment*, revised 10th anniversary ed. London: Routledge.

Collins, P. H., & Bilge, S. (2016). *Intersectionality.* Cambridge; Malden, MA: Polity Press.

Conradson, D., & Latham, A. (2005a). Transnational urbanism: Attending to everyday practices and mobilities. *Journal of Ethnic and Migration Studies*, 31(2), 227–233. doi:10.1080/1369183042000339891.

Conradson, D., & Latham, A. (2005b). Friendship, networks and transnationality in a world city: Antipodean transmigrants in London. *Journal of Ethnic and Migration Studies*, 31(2), 287–305. doi:10.1080/1369183042000339936.

Conradson, D., & Latham, A. (2005c). Escalator London? A case study of New Zealand tertiary educated migrants in a global city. *Journal of Contemporary European Studies*, 13(2), 159–172. doi:10.1080/14782800500212376.

Crossley, N. (2010). *Towards relational sociology.* London: Routledge.

Das, R. (2019). *Early motherhood in digital societies: Ideals, anxieties and ties of the perinatal.* London: Routledge.

Department of Home Affairs. (2018). Australia's 2019–20 migration program (Discussion Paper). Retrieved from http://scoa.org.au/wp-content/uploads/2019/01/discussion-paper-australias-2019-20-migration.pdf.

DeSouza, R. (2005). Transforming possibilities of care: Goan migrant motherhood in New Zealand. *Contemporary Nurse: A Journal for the Australian Nursing Profession*, 20, 87–101. doi:10.5172/conu.20.1.87.

De Winter, J., Kocurek, C. A., & Vie, S. (2017). Managing community managers: Social labor, feminized skills, and professionalization. *Communication Design Quarterly Review*, 4(4), 36–45. doi:10.1145/3071088.3071092.

Diminescu, D. (2008). The connected migrant: An epistemological manifesto. *Social Science Information*, 47(4), 565–579.

Djurdjevic, M., & Roca Girona, J. (2016). Mixed couples and critical cosmopolitanism: Experiences of cross-border love. *Journal of Intercultural Studies*, 37(4), 390–405. doi:10.1080/07256868.2016.1190695.

Doucet, A. (1998). Interpreting mother-work: Linking methodology, ontology, theory and personal biography. *Canadian Woman Studies*, 18(2/3), 52.

Douglas, S. J., & Michaels, M. W. (2004). *The mommy myth: The idealization of motherhood and how it has undermined all women*. Free Press.

Dwyer, S. C., & Buckle, J. L. (2009). The space between: On being an insider-outsider in qualitative research. *International Journal of Qualitative Methods*, 8(1), 54–63. doi:10.1177/160940690900800105.

Ebaugh, H. R., & Curry, M. (2000). Fictive kin as social capital in new immigrant communities. *Sociological Perspectives*, 43(2), 189–209. doi:10.2307/1389793.

Edwards, A. E. (2000). Community mothering: The relationship between mothering and the community work of Black women. *Journal of the Motherhood Initiative for Research and Community Involvement*, 2(2), 87–100.

Eysenbach, G., & Till, J. E. (2001). Ethical issues in qualitative research on internet communities. *BMJ*, 323(7321), 1103–1105. doi:10.1136/bmj.323.7321.1103.

Ferreday, D. (2013). Afterword: Digital relationships and feminist hope. In K. Orton-Johnson, & N. Prior (Eds.), *Digital sociology: Critical perspectives* (pp. 51–57). London: Palgrave Macmillan.

Francisco, V. (2015). 'The internet is magic': Technology, intimacy and transnational families. *Critical Sociology*, 41(1), 173–190. doi:10.1177/0896920513484602.

Francisco-Menchavez, V. (2018). *The labor of care: Filipina migrants and transnational families in the digital age*. Urbana: University of Illinois Press.

Fresnoza-Flot, A. (2009). Migration status and transnational mothering: The case of Filipino migrants in France. *Global Networks*, 9(2), 252–270. doi:10.1111/j.1471-0374.2009.00253.x.

Gatt, S., Hazibar, K., Sauermann, V., Preglau, M., & Ralser, M. (2016). Migration from a gender-critical, postcolonial and interdisciplinary perspective. *Österreichische Zeitschrift für Soziologie*, 41(3), 1–12. doi:10.1007/s11614-016-0236-4.

Gedalof, I. (2009). Birth, belonging and migrant mothers: Narratives of reproduction in feminist migration studies. *Feminist Review*, 93(1), 81–100. doi:10.1057/fr.2009.23.

Gilmartin, M., & Migge, B. (2016). Migrant mothers and the geographies of belonging. *Gender, Place & Culture*, 23(2), 147–161. doi:10.1080/0966369X.2014.991700.

Goodwin, S., & Huppatz, K. (2010). *The good mother: Contemporary motherhoods in Australia*. Sydney, NSW: Sydney University Press.

Hage, G. (1997). At home in the entrails of the west. In H. Grace, G. Hage, L. Johnson, J. Langsworth, & M. Symonds (Eds.), *Home/world: Space, community and marginality in Sydney's west* (pp. 99–153). Annandale, NSW: Pluto Press.

Haraway, D. (1988). Situated knowledges: The science question in feminism and the privilege of partial perspective. *Feminist Studies*, 14(3), 575–599.

Haraway, D. (1991). A cyborg manifesto: Science, technology, and socialist-feminism in the late twentieth century. In D. Haraway (Ed.), *Simians, cyborgs, and women: The reinvention of nature*. London: Free Association Books.

Harding, S. (2004). *The feminist standpoint theory reader: Intellectual and political controversies*. New York: Routledge.

Hawkesworth, M. E. (2006). *Feminist inquiry: From political conviction to methodological innovation*. New Brunswick, NJ: Rutgers University Press.

Hicks, M. (2010, 7/10/2010). New groups: Stay closer to groups of people in your life. Retrieved from https://www.facebook.com/notes/facebook/new-groups-stay-clo ser-to-groups-of-people-in-your-life/434700832130.

Hiller, H. H., & McCaig, K. S. (2007). Reassessing the role of partnered women in migration decision-making and migration outcomes. *Journal of Social and Personal Relationships*, 24(3), 457–472. doi:10.1177/0265407507077233.

Hine, C. (2015). *Ethnography for the internet: Embedded, embodied and everyday*. London: Bloomsbury Publishing.

Ho, C. (2006). Migration as feminisation? Chinese women's experiences of work and family in Australia. *Journal of Ethnic and Migration Studies*, 32(3), 497–514.

Ho, E. L.-E. (2011). Migration trajectories of 'highly skilled' middling transnationals: Singaporean transmigrants in London. *Population, Space and Place*, 17(1), 116–129. doi:10.1002/psp.569.

Hoban, E., & Liamputtong, P. (2012). Cambodian migrant women's postpartum experiences in Victoria, Australia. *Midwifery*, 29(7), 772–778. doi:10.1016/j.midw.2012.06.021.

Hondagneu-Sotelo, P. (1994). *Gendered transitions: Mexican experiences of immigration*. University of California Press.

Hondagneu-Sotelo, P., & Avila, E. (1997). "I'm here but I'm there": The meanings of Latina transnational motherhood. *Gender & Society*, 11(5), 548–571. doi:10.1177/089124397011005003.

Hudson, J. M., & Bruckman, A. (2004). "Go away": Participant objections to being studied and the ethics of chatroom research. *The Information Society*, 20(2), 127–139. doi:10.1080/01972240490423030.

Hugo, G. (2006). Temporary migration and the labour market in Australia. *Australian Geographer*, 37(2), 211–231. doi:10.1080/00049180600672359.

Hunt, E. (2017, 27/06/2017). Barely half of population born in Australia to Australian-born parents. *The Guardian*. Retrieved from https://www.theguardian.com/australia-news/ 2017/jun/27/australia-reaches-tipping-point-with-quarter-of-population-born-overseas.

Jarrett, K. (2016). *Feminism, labour and digital media: The digital housewife*. New York: Routledge.

Jin, K.-X. (2017). Our first communities summit and new tools for group admins. Retrieved from https://newsroom.fb.com/news/2017/06/our-first-communities-summ it-and-new-tools-for-group-admins/.

Johnson, A., Lawson, C., & Ames, K. (2018). *'Are you one of us?': The ethics of research in a private Facebook community*. Proceedings of the 9th International Conference on Social Media and Society, pp. 102–109.

Johnson, S. (2015). 'Intimate mothering publics': Comparing face-to-face support groups and internet use for women seeking information and advice in the transition to first-time motherhood. *Culture, Health & Sexuality*, 17(2), 237–251. doi:10.1080/13691058.2014.968807.

Jupp, J. (2001). *The Australian people: An encyclopedia of the nation, its people and their origins* (Vol. 2). Cambridge University Press.

Kanno, Y., & Norton, B. (2003). Imagined communities and educational possibilities: Introduction. *Journal of Language, Identity & Education*, 2(4), 241–249. doi:10.1207/ S15327701JLIE0204_1.

King, S. A. (1996). Researching internet communities: Proposed ethical guidelines for the reporting of results. *The Information Society*, 12(2), 119–128. doi:10.1080/713856145.

Komito, L., & Bates, J. (2012). Migration, community and social media. In G. Boucher, A. Grindsted, & T. L. Vicente (Eds.), *Transnationalism in the global city* (pp. 97–112). Bilbao: Universidad de Deusto.

Kozinets, R. V. (2015). Netnography. In *The international encyclopedia of digital communication and society*. John Wiley & Sons, Inc.

Lennon, K. (2015). *Imagination and the imaginary*. London; New York: Routledge.

Leurs, K., & Ponzanesi, S. (2018). Connected migrants: Encapsulation and cosmopolitanization. *Popular Communication*, 16(1), 4–20. doi:10.1080/15405702.2017.1418359.

Liamputtong, P. (2006). Motherhood and "moral career": Discourses of good motherhood among Southeast Asian immigrant women in Australia. *Qualitative Sociology*, 29(1), 25–53. doi:10.1007/s11133-005-9006-5.

Lupton, D., Pedersen, S., & Thomas, G. M. (2016). Parenting and digital media: From the early web to contemporary digital society. *Sociology Compass*, 10(8), 730–743. doi:10.1111/soc4.12398.

Luthra, R., & Platt, L. (2016). Elite or middling? International students and migrant diversification. *Ethnicities*, 16(2), 316–344. doi:10.1177/1468796815616155.

Madianou, M. (2012). Migration and the accentuated ambivalence of motherhood: The role of ICTs in Filipino transnational families. *Global Networks*, 12(3), 277–295. doi:10.1111/j.1471-0374.2012.00352.x.

Manohar, N. N. (2013a). Mothering for class and ethnicity: The case of Indian professional immigrants in the United States. *Advances in Gender Research*, 17, 159–185. doi:10.1108/S1529-2126(2013)0000017011.

Manohar, N. N. (2013b). Support networks, ethnic spaces, and fictive kin: Indian immigrant women constructing community in the United States. *AAPI Nexus: Policy, Practice and Community*, 11(1–2), 25–55. doi:10.17953/appc.11.1-2.t81xj18224638u44.

Manohar, N. N. (2013c). 'Yes you're Tamil! But are you Tamil enough?' An Indian researcher interrogates 'shared social location' in feminist immigration research. *International Journal of Multiple Research Approaches*, 7(2), 189–203. doi:10.5172/mra.2013.7.2.189.

Manohar, N. N., & Busse-Cárdenas, E. (2011). Valuing "good" motherhood in migration: The experiences of Indian professional wives in America and Peruvian working-class wives left behind in Peru. *Journal of the Motherhood Initiative for Research and Community Involvement*, 2(2), 175–195.

Mares, P. (2017). *Not quite Australian: How temporary migration is changing the nation*. Text Publishing Company.

Meyers, C., & Rugunanan, P. (2020). Mobile-mediated mothering from a distance: A case study of Somali mothers in Port Elizabeth, South Africa. *International Journal of Cultural Studies*, 23(5), 656–673. doi:10.1177/1367877920926645.

Mullings, B. (1999). Insider or outsider, both or neither: Some dilemmas of interviewing in a crosscultural setting. *Geoforum*, 30(4), 337–350.

Nedelsky, J. (2011). *Law's relations: A relational theory of self, autonomy, and law*. New York: Oxford University Press.

Nissenbaum, H. (2011). A contextual approach to privacy online. *Daedalus*, 140(4), 32–48. doi:10.1162/DAED_a_00113.

O'Reilly, A. (2009). *Maternal thinking: Philosophy, politics, practice*. Bradford, ON: Demeter Press.

O'Reilly, A. (2016). *Matricentric feminism: Theory, activism, practice.* Bradford, ON: Demeter Press.

Parreñas, R. S. (2001). Mothering from a distance: Emotions, gender, and intergenerational relations in Filipino transnational families. *Feminist Studies,* 27(2), 361–390.

Parreñas, R. S. (2014). The intimate labour of transnational communication. *Families, Relationships and Societies,* 3(3), 425–442. doi:10.1332/204674313X13802800868637.

Peng, Y., & Wong, O. M. H. (2013). Diversified transnational mothering via telecommunication: Intensive, collaborative, and passive. *Gender & Society,* 27(4), 491–513. doi:10.1177/0891243212473197.

Pessar, P. (1999). Engendering migration studies: The case of new immigrants in the United States. *American Behavioral Scientist,* 42(4), 577–600. doi:10.1177/00027649921 954372.

Portes, A., & Zhou, M. (1992). Gaining the upper hand: Economic mobility among immigrant and domestic minorities. *Ethnic and Racial Studies,* 15(4), 491–522. doi:10.1080/01419870.1992.9993761.

Portwood-Stacer, L. (2014). Care work and the stakes of social media refusal. *New Criticals.* http://www.newcriticals.com/care-work-and-the-stakes-of-social-media-refusal/print.

Prandini, R. (2015). Relational sociology: A well-defined sociological paradigm or a challenging 'relational turn' in sociology? *International Review of Sociology,* 25(1), 1–14. doi:10.1080/03906701.2014.997969.

Raphael, D. (1975). Matrescence, becoming a mother, a new/old rite de passage. In *Being female: Reproduction, power, and change.* Berkeley: University of California.

Renzaho, A. M. N., & Oldroyd, J. C. (2014). Closing the gap in maternal and child health: A qualitative study examining health needs of migrant mothers in Dandenong, Victoria, Australia. *Maternal and Child Health Journal,* 18(6), 1391–1402. doi:10.1007/s10995-013-1378-7.

Reynolds, T., & Erel, U. (2018). Migrant mothers: Kin work and cultural work in making future citizens. *Families, Relationships and Societies,* 7(3), 357–363. doi:10.1332/204674318X15384702898352.

Roulston, K. J. (2008). Conversational interviewing. In L. Given (Ed.), *The SAGE encyclopedia of qualitative research methods* (pp. 127–129). Thousand Oaks, CA.

Ruddick, S. (1980). Maternal thinking. *Feminist Studies,* 6(2), 342–367. doi:10.2307/3177749.

Ruddick, S. (1989). *Maternal thinking: Toward a politics of peace.* Boston: Beacon Press.

Ryan, L. (2008). Navigating the emotional terrain of families "here" and "there": Women, migration and the management of emotions. *Journal of Intercultural Studies,* 29(3), 299–313. doi:10.1080/07256860802169238.

Rzepnikowska, A. (2019). *Convivial cultures in multicultural cities: Polish migrant women in Manchester and Barcelona.* London: Routledge.

Silvey, R. (2004). Power, difference and mobility: Feminist advances in migration studies. *Progress in Human Geography,* 28(4), 490–506.

Singh, S. (2016). *Money, migration, and family.* New York: Palgrave Macmillan.

Sun, N., Rau, P. P.-L., & Ma, L. (2014). Understanding lurkers in online communities: A literature review. *Computers in Human Behavior,* 38, 110–117. doi:10.1016/j.chb.2014.05.022.

Thurer, S. (1995). *The myths of motherhood: How culture reinvents the good mother.* New York: Penguin (Original work published 1994).

Tobin, C., Murphy-Lawless, J., & Beck, C. T. (2014). Childbirth in exile: Asylum seeking women's experience of childbirth in Ireland. *Midwifery*, 30(7), 831–838. doi:10.1016/j.midw.2013.07.012.

Utomo, A. (2014). Mother tongue, mothering, and (transnational) identity: Indonesian mothers in Canberra, Australia. *ASEAS – Austrian Journal of South-East Asian Studies*, 7(2), 165–182. doi:10.14764/10.ASEAS-2014.2-3.

Valentine, G. (2002). People like us: Negotiating sameness and difference in the research process. In P. Moss (Ed.), *Feminist geography in practice: Research and methods* (pp. 116–126). Oxford: Blackwell.

Wilding, R., Baldassar, L., Gamage, S., Worrell, S., & Mohamud, S. (2020). Digital media and the affective economies of transnational families. *International Journal of Cultural Studies*, 23(5), 639–655. doi:10.1177/1367877920920278.

Williams Veazey, L. (2016). Mothering in the digital diaspora. In L. B. Arnold, & B. Martin (Eds.), *Taking the village online: Mothers, motherhood, and social media* (pp. 81–97). Bradford, ON: Demeter Press.

Williams Veazey, L. (2019). Glocalised motherhood: Sociality and affect in migrant mothers' online communities. *Feminist Encounters: A Journal of Critical Studies in Culture and Politics*, 3(1–2), 1–15. doi:10.20897/femenc/5915.

Williams Veazey, L. (2020). Migrant mothers and the ambivalence of co-ethnicity in online communities. *Journal of Ethnic and Migration Studies*. doi:10.1080/1369183X.2020.1782180.

Wong, S.-L., & Salaff, J. (1998). Network capital: Emigration from Hong Kong. *British Journal of Sociology*, 49(3), 358–374. doi:10.2307/591388.

Yang, X., Li, G., & Huang, S. S. (2017). Perceived online community support, member relations, and commitment: Differences between posters and lurkers. *Information & Management*, 54(2), 154–165. doi:10.1016/j.im.2016.05.003.

Yelland, J., Riggs, E., Small, R., & Brown, S. (2015). Maternity services are not meeting the needs of immigrant women of non-English speaking background: Results of two consecutive Australian population based studies. *Midwifery*, 31(7), 664–670. doi:10.1016/j.midw.2015.03.001.

2 Migrant maternal online communities

Introduction

Lina

Newly arrived in Sydney, Lina[1] *drove to IKEA to buy some essential items to set up her new home. When her baby's nappy needed changing, she went to the toilets, where she overheard some women speaking Swedish. "I knew I wanted to meet some Swedish mums," she says, "and here they were, in the toilets at IKEA, of course!" Lina quickly asked the women how they knew each other, and whether there was some kind of Swedish mothers' group she could join. They told her about a Facebook group for Swedish mothers in her area. The group had been set up by Eva about six months earlier, to make it easier for her small network of Swedish mothers to meet up. The group initially formed through individual connections ("I knew two Swedes, and they knew someone, and they knew someone, so I think we were six people," Eva explained) and met weekly in their local park. The women would chat, in Swedish, about life as new mothers living far from home. They hoped to expose their children to the Swedish language and to other Swedish families. The group's online presence enabled more women to find the group, extending it beyond the existing social networks of the founding members.*

After about a year, the park meet-ups dwindled as some women returned to work, their children's activities changed, and their friendships matured and became less dependent on the group. Some of the women chose to send their children to the same preschool, to maintain the connections made through the group. Others continue to meet to celebrate birthdays or Swedish Midsummer parties. The online platform has enabled the group to grow alongside the original members' growing children, welcoming new members as they arrive in Sydney and find the group. At the time of the interviews, the online group was mostly used for coordinating Swedish celebrations, providing information to new migrants, and buying and selling Swedish items, such as books, clothes, or furniture. "I guess it's a sentimental, emotional thing, just to have a bit of Sweden with you," Eva explains, "And it's easier to sell to other Swedes, obviously."

This chapter introduces the phenomenon and context of the migrant maternal Facebook groups at the heart of this study.[2] First, the defining features of the groups are explained before being placed in the broader context and history of parents' groups in Australia. Secondly, the origins of the groups are explained in relation to the personal mothering and migration stories of the women who created them, and in the context of the rising popularity of Facebook groups. Finally, the chapter outlines the main activities undertaken in the groups, focusing on the exchange of information and the ways in which this exchange is part of a social strategy undertaken by women in an attempt to navigate their lives as migrant mothers in Australia.

This chapter draws on concepts of identity and boundaries to explore how the parameters of the groups are shaped by their creators. This discussion is extended by introducing notions of privacy, publicness, and visibility in social networks and online groups. To conceptualise the social, informational, and affective interchanges that occur under the auspices of the migrant maternal online communities, I draw on concepts from information grounds theory (Fisher & Naumer 2006; Pettigrew 1999) and the notion of "social information foraging" (Pirolli 2009) in online contexts.

I interviewed women from fourteen Facebook groups created by and for migrant mothers: six Sydney-based groups, seven Melbourne-based groups,[3] and one Australia-wide group. The smallest group had 21 online members at the time of the interview, and the largest had nearly 5,000. The longest running group had been created in 2009, while the most recently formed was established in December 2015 and quickly grew to become the largest group in the study.[4] Table A.1 (Appendix 1) presents an overview of the groups involved in the interview phase and the members who were interviewed.

Creating the groups

One of the first acts when setting up a Facebook group is to decide on a name. In so doing, the creator sets expectations about who they envisage joining the group and what they might use it for. From a potential member's perspective, the group name signals whether they will be welcome and might find what they need there. All the groups in this research included the following identifiers:

- *Origin* referent (country, region, linguistic group)[5]
- *Role* referent (mother, parent, or family)
- *Residence* referent (sub-metropolitan area, city, country)

Choices and negotiations around naming practices worked to produce particular migrant maternal identities. Sabina drew on regionally based historical, linguistic, and cultural commonalities to explain her decision to create a group for Scandinavian, rather than Swedish, mothers. The Spanish-speaking group used language as their origin referent, welcoming members from both

Europe and South America. Groups that had been created as singularly British, or Indian, had responded to requests from members to expand the parameters to include Irish and other South Asian mothers respectively. These members had friends who wanted to join the groups and understood themselves to have similar needs and experiences.

In joining the groups, women encountered and negotiated the complexities of their own migrant maternal identities. Celine, a woman with dual French-English heritage, migrated from England and gave birth to both her children in New Zealand before moving to Sydney. At first, Celine identified with other women who had migrated with their young families from New Zealand to Australia, noting, "I've never been a British mum. I've been a Kiwi mum, despite sounding like I'm English." After joining groups for British and New Zealand mothers in Sydney, however, Celine felt she had more in common with the British mothers, based on her impression of their class and education, as displayed in online posts, and the suburbs they lived in. Kavita, a British migrant with Indian heritage, joined separate groups for British and Indian mothers in Sydney. Maria, the Colombian administrator of the Spanish-speaking group, had also joined a Brazilian mothers' group and found it to be more useful to her than the group she ran. Creating, joining, and shaping the groups provided an opportunity for migrant mothers to claim, negotiate, and re-shape individual and collective identities. Through these negotiations, the women construct common-sense understandings of identity, re-working "imagined communities" (Anderson 2006 [1983]) by deploying pragmatic and emotional understandings of national and regional identities, shared histories, and language.

The role referent, referring to members' roles as mothers, parents, or family members, was also not straightforward. Two groups (one Swedish, one German) were open to men and women, and included terms like "parents" or "families" in their group name. All others used a word relating to "mother" in the name. In practice, six groups included only mothers and enforced this policy.[6] Three said they would welcome fathers into the group, despite being named as a mothers' group.[7] The remaining two groups were strictly for women only and retained a focus on mothering but were open to (female) nannies, for example, or any woman with an interest in joining.[8] One group from the mapping exercise justified their use of the term "mum" as a more effective search term, noting in their public information: "It's called Irish Mums because that's what most people would search for but we recognise that lots of dads do the primary care."[9] No groups exclusively for migrant fathers were identified at this stage.[10]

None of the groups from the interview phase used the term 'migrant' in their name, and although most were aimed at people who had moved from one country to another, some also included the children of migrants, spouses of migrants, and those with an affiliation for the 'origin referent' via heritage or affection. Some administrators noted a tension between, on the one hand, creating a sense of locally based belonging by insisting members currently reside in the specified area and, on the other, providing a useful service for prospective migrants.

Privacy and disclosure in closed Facebook groups

Facebook has three group settings: public, closed, and secret. All groups involved in interviews, and most in the mapping exercise, operated as closed groups. Any Facebook user can see a closed group's name and description but only members can view content posted in the group. Content posted in public Facebook groups are visible to any user, while secret groups do not appear in search results and thus would not have been included in the study. Closed groups require an administrator to approve each new member. Administrators can edit and delete posts, set group rules, remove and 'mute' members, change the group's name, close or archive the group, and so on. Administrators in closed groups therefore play a significant role in the creation, curation, and maintenance of the groups. Of the 41 migrant mothers interviewed, 15 held an administrator role.

Research on Facebook predominantly focuses on its social networking functionality, revolving around a personal profile and linked network of 'friends' (for example, d. boyd 2010; Chambers 2017). Less commonly researched are the other features, such as groups, which enable users to interact with people beyond their 'friend' network, in bounded spaces in the Facebook environment.[11] Facebook's emphasis on using 'real names' and privacy settings to manage disclosure and protection of personal information means that the migrant maternal groups in this study function differently from the web-based forums on which much previous online mothering research has been based, where content is often publicly visible, with members using pseudonyms (usernames) to maintain some degree of privacy (for example, Jensen 2013; Madge & O'Connor 2006; Pedersen & Lupton 2018). The Groups functionality is one way to manage the "context collapse" noted by many social media researchers (J. L. Davis & Jurgenson 2014; Ellison et al. 2011; Marwick & boyd 2011), in which a person's otherwise segmented social network – family, friends, colleagues, acquaintances – "converge into a single mass" (J. L. Davis & Jurgenson 2014, p. 478) and complicate an individual's ability to manage self-presentation and "identity performance" (p. 477). Groups are an increasingly popular means of managing a central tension in social media use: the desire to balance privacy concerns with opportunities to gain social capital through self-disclosure (Ellison et al. 2011).

Groups enable users to segment their networks and seek specific resources and relationships (social capital) from specific audiences. For example, Katrin can discuss her struggles with homesickness in a closed group without that discussion being visible to her mother or work colleagues; and Petra can discuss her husband's lack of support for her aspiration to teach their child German without it being visible to her husband or his family. Conversely, women in the groups can draw on each other for support and information without the personal disclosures involved in becoming 'Facebook friends' (Chambers 2013, p. 47). Using groups in this way is a "privacy-protective strategy" deployed by mothers to facilitate "access to the benefits of open discussion while mitigating the risk of revealing too much information to inappropriate audiences" (Chalklen & Anderson 2017, p. 2).

Context: Mothers' groups in Australia

These migrant maternal Facebook groups should be seen in the context of online and offline mothers' groups operating in Australia and many other parts of the world. In Australia, state-supported mothers' groups have played a prominent role in the lives of new mothers for around a century. Nurse-run groups and baby clinics were established in Australia in the early twentieth century to educate new mothers and reduce infant mortality rates (Barnes et al. 2003, pp. 14–15). The 1970s saw a change to a more socially oriented service, providing information and social interaction to support mothers in their new role (Barnes et al. 2003, p. 15; J. S. Lawson & Callaghan 1991, p. 64). Despite an official shift in 1997 to the gender-neutral term "parents' groups," these groups are still commonly referred to as "mothers' groups" (see, for example, Cameron et al. 2019), and research focuses almost exclusively on mothers' experiences of these groups (Strange et al. 2014).

In the states of New South Wales and Victoria, Maternal and Child Health Services commonly facilitate five to eight group sessions for new parents (NSW Health 2010). Many parents continue to meet afterwards, creating "self-sustaining supportive social networks" (Scott et al. 2001, p. 24; Lawson & Callaghan 1991, p. 65). Studies suggest participants value the "mothercraft" and "companionship" aspects of the programme (Lawson & Callaghan 1991, p. 65), the chance to share experiences of motherhood, receive peer support, and the opportunity for their children to socialise (Scott et al. 2001, p. 28). Mothers' groups increase mothers' sense of connection to their local community (Strange et al. 2014), but migrant mothers, particularly those with less English fluency, may be missing out on the benefits of universal services such as mothers' groups and playgroups (Scott et al. 2001, p. 26).

Local support for migrant mothers in Australia

Playgroups are used by state and community groups to support the settlement of newly arrived migrants. Both Playgroup Australia and government Early Childhood Services provide specific support targeted at migrant mothers, and parents from culturally and linguistically diverse backgrounds. Not-for-profit organisations, such as Settlement Services International and Save the Children, and religious groups, organise playgroups for new migrants, sometimes in conjunction with Playgroup Australia affiliates (Jesuit Refugee Service Australia 2015; Playgroup NSW 2017; Settlement Services International 2017). Community groups, like the Mums 4 Refugees collective, coordinate volunteers to help run playgroups for newly arrived migrants (Canterbury City Community Centre 2017). Research suggests such playgroups help migrants to overcome social isolation and adjust to Australian parenting cultures and laws, and support children's social and physical development (Commerford & Robinson 2016; Warr et al. 2013). Playgroups also provide "a soft entry point to the service system" (VICSEG New Futures 2014, p. 2; see also Commerford & Robinson 2016), encouraging migrants to access other support services such as language classes. The peer-led mothers' groups in this study, some of which have initiated playgroups as part of their activities, are not typically included in research about services for migrant mothers and children because they are not affiliated with institutions of state or civil society.

Playgroups targeted at migrant families help to overcome some of the barriers migrants face in accessing generic groups. Research suggests that fluency in English is associated with better rates of attendance at mothers' groups and playgroups (Gregory et al. 2016, p. 21; D. Scott et al. 2001, p. 26). In addition, Warr et al. (2013) point to barriers such as prioritising meeting essential needs such as housing and food, lack of access to transport, feelings of physical insecurity, distrust of services and government intervention coupled with an unfamiliarity with the playgroup concept, and gender roles where women might need to seek permission from their husband to attend. The same research highlights the importance of the playgroup facilitators, themselves migrants, in encouraging families to attend, setting the affective atmosphere of the group, modelling unfamiliar parenting techniques, and providing trusted information (p. 45–46). Their role involves many hours of unpaid practical and emotional work, providing practical assistance, facilitating social connections, "managing inter-personal tensions that erupted in playgroups from time to time" (p. 46), and playing a bridging role between the migrants and state services. This finding resonates with the findings of this study around the significant role of the administrators, which is explored in Chapter 4.

Online mothers' groups

A significant body of research since the late 1990s has explored mothers' experiences of using online mothering communities (for example, Arnold 2011; K. E. Davis 2015; Drentea & Moren-Cross 2005, 2011; Dunham et al. 1998; Gibson & Hanson 2013; Jensen 2013; Johnson 2015; J. Kim et al. 2015; Madge & O'Connor 2004, 2005, 2006). Echoing the research cited above concerning offline mothers' groups, studies of online mothers' groups tend to emphasise their importance for information, social interaction, and maternal role development. In contrast to the historical aim of offline mothers' groups – to inculcate norms of maternal practice – some studies of online mothers' groups note their potential to act as sites of resistance to gendered, unequal, and intensive parenting norms (Arnold 2011; Drentea & Moren-Cross 2005; Jensen 2013; Johnson 2015; Madge & O'Connor 2006). Existing research into online mothers' communities has tended to focus on web-based forum platforms often attached to a parenting website, such as BabyCenter. This reflects the dominance of such platforms in the 1990s and 2000s and the later development of Facebook Groups as a platform for mothering communities.

Facebook groups for mothers have grown in popularity in recent years. In Australia, Facebook groups for mothers in Sydney's North Shore and Inner West areas, for example, had over 30,000 and 22,000 members respectively by the end of 2018 (North Shore Mums 2018; Inner West Mums 2018). The Facebook groups for migrant mothers in this study were mostly established around the same time as these generic mothers' groups (2012 onwards), and some were directly inspired by them. Many of the research participants were members of multiple online mothers' groups and networks across Facebook, forums, and other platforms, and many had also attended a local, nurse-led mothers' group. The migrant maternal Facebook groups form part of a landscape of online and offline mothering communities, and the mothers' use of groups across the various modes and platforms informs their expectations and usage of these specific groups.

Origins of the groups: Chronology

The groups in the study were all created between 2009 and 2015; mostly between 2012 and 2014. This period coincides with the introduction of a re-designed Groups tool on Facebook in October 2010. Although groups had existed on Facebook before, the re-designed functionality was explicitly designed "to make sharing and communication with small groups of people easier" (Hicks 2010). In 2017, Facebook announced new tools for group administrators, noting the centrality of groups to Facebook's corporate mission (Jin 2017). Between 2010 and 2017, therefore, the participation in Facebook groups became much more commonplace alongside users' individual profiles and friendship networks. The development of the migrant maternal groups in this study should be considered in this changing context. Few of the participants embarked on both their migration and motherhood journeys accompanied by these Facebook groups. In many cases, their migration and/or transition to motherhood preceded the existence of (or their knowledge of) the groups.

Of the thirteen women who created groups, three did so in the first two years of arriving in Australia and about half started their group within five years of arrival. Priya, Nicole, and Yasmin created their groups 13, 15, and 26 years respectively after their migration to Australia. Viewed in relation to their motherhood journey, three women started groups shortly after their first child's birth, six around the time of their second child's birth, and one between the birth of her first and second children. Of the remaining three, two migrated with older children and set up a group soon after their arrival, and Jenni was asked by the Swedish Church to set up the Swedish parents' group before she became a mother. Therefore, most groups were set up either soon after the administrator's arrival in Australia or in the years around the birth of their children, or both. They were all created when the Facebook Groups functionality was being developed and promoted as a central plank of their corporate strategy. That some women chose to create groups many years after migration suggests that the condition of being a mother away from 'home' may remain a salient source of identity beyond an initial settlement period, and that migrant mothers may desire contact with others with a similar experience or identity even many years after migration. Indeed, the significant life change involved in the transition to motherhood may inspire a renewed interest in such connections. One explanation for the association between group creation and the birth of a second child could be that state-supported mothers' groups are often restricted to first-time mothers (or parents) (Strange et al. 2014, p. 2841). Those who have experienced the support of a mothers' group, finding themselves excluded from the state-run provision, might consider setting up a version of their own.

Origins of the groups: Precedents

The availability, popularity, convenience, and ease of use of Facebook groups coincided with these participants' need for support and connection. Historical and contemporary precedents for maternally focused support groups, and the increasing use of online social networks by migrants, also shaped the conditions in which these groups were created. Nisha's decision to create the groups for South Asian mothers in Melbourne was influenced by a wealth of contemporary and historical precedents. Nisha grew up in an Indian army family and recalled the importance of the support networks formed by the wives and mothers during the men's absence. When she had her first child in the United States, she joined a network of Indian mother bloggers and drew on them for support, particularly in the absence of her own mother, who had died before Nisha had children. One of those bloggers met Nisha in Melbourne, shortly after she moved there, providing a point of social continuity during the upheaval of migration. She used an Indian online parenting site with a section for Indian mothers overseas and used MeetUp.com to find other Indian parents in her US city. For Nisha, the potential of female-focused networks was well-established, and in Melbourne in 2014, she chose a Facebook group as the platform on which to launch the one she needed. Locally based Facebook groups for mothers in Australia were gaining popularity at that time. Aditi, Yasmin, Rebecca, and Sabina were all inspired by their local mothers' Facebook groups in Sydney and Melbourne to set up groups to meet their specific needs as migrant mothers. Yasmin was also inspired by her local nurse-led mothers' group and hoped to replicate the experience of her "Australian mothers' group" but with local Persian mothers. Face-to-face mothers' groups were also a key mechanism by which participants learned of the existence of the online groups.

Indian mothers in Sydney: From events committee to culturally sensitive support community

In 2014, a member of a Sydney mothers' Facebook group proposed a playgroup for mothers of Indian heritage. In response to claims by some group members that this constituted "reverse racism," others organised a 'Bollywood night' to reaffirm their commitment to cultural diversity, bring people together, and raise money for a women's health charity (Nicastri 2014; Walther 2014). *To assist in organising future events, the event's organising committee suggested setting up a local Indian mothers' Facebook group. The group was set up in October 2015 and quickly grew to 80 members. The administrators decided to open the group to Indian mothers in the whole of Sydney, not just in the original group of suburbs: "We thought, we are such a minority in Sydney, why do we want to create further divisions […]?" Administrators encouraged members to add their friends and offered small incentives such as prize draws. The group grew to 1,000 members in a few months. Two years later, the group had over 16,000 members, by far the largest group in this study.*[12] *From its origins as an events committee, the group has developed into a "culturally sensitive" support community for Indian mothers in Sydney. Aditi, the administrator interviewed for this study, is proud of having created "a portal for Indian women" where they can talk, get "culturally sensitive advice," and meet each other. "People have made friends, made friends for their kids; they can meet like-minded people, you know, just a sense of belonging."*

Introducing the participants

The 41 research participants were all mothers, ranging in age from 30 to 49. 35 of them had had their first child while living in a migrant context.[13] Four had teenaged children, but most had younger children. Excluding the teenagers and babies in utero, the average age of participants' children was four years old at the time of interview. 37 women had arrived in Australia since 2000, 19 of whom had arrived since 2010. So, the average participant had one or two young children and had arrived seven to ten years prior to the interviews. All the participants in this research were women who had given birth to their children and had been responsible for their care since their birth and during pregnancy. Most lived in nuclear family arrangements with their children and partner, although some participants had experience of living in extended family settings (with parents, parents-in-law, or other relatives) either in their country of origin or in Australia. One divorced participant lived alone with her children.

All the women were, or had been, in long-term partnerships (mostly marriages) with men. Two-thirds of the participants were in a relationship with another migrant, and three-quarters of these (n=20) had migrated to Australia together. The remaining third were in relationships with Australian men, and half of those couples had met overseas and subsequently migrated to Australia. These permutations of relationship, migration, and motherhood were unevenly distributed across the groups. For example, five out of the eight participants from the Sydney-based German group had Australian partners, and four of those five were living in the specific area of Sydney where their partner had grown up. This meant that they mostly had access to some element of family support, and to their partner's friendship network, and proximity to knowledge about Australian systems. On the other hand, they sometimes felt isolated from their own culture and solely responsible for teaching their child to speak German and facilitating relationships with their German relatives. In addition, most of them felt they had little choice but to remain in Australia, with no prospect of returning 'home' due to their husband's reluctance to live and work in a non-Anglophone country. All participants from this group, whether in relationships to Australian or German men, had become mothers after they migrated.

By contrast, all the Indian-born participants from the Sydney-based Indian group were married to Indian men.[14] Three had migrated with their Indian husbands, two had migrated on spousal visas to join husbands who had already settled in Australia, and one had migrated as a secondary applicant on her husband's work visa but had remained in India for her pregnancy and the birth of their child, due to their ineligibility for public healthcare on his visa. In these migrant/migrant couples, the women had less access to ongoing, co-present family support, although most experienced extended visits from parents and/or parents-in-law, especially around the time of the birth of their children. Most women also made extended visits to India with their young child(ren). As a family, they had less information and knowledge about Australian health and education systems and initially had little access to friendship networks beyond work colleagues. On the other hand, they tended to be less anxious about passing down their home language, values, and culture, as this could be achieved within the home environment.[15] These patterns in family formation are broadly reflected in the national census data. While 55% of Swedish and 46% of German migrants with a spouse or partner are in relationships with Australian-born partners, the figures are 4% for partnered Indian migrants, 7% for Iranian migrants, and 25% for Brazilian migrants (Australian Bureau of Statistics 2017).[16]

Simran

Simran arrived in Sydney six months before our interview. She migrated from India with her baby, joining her husband who had been working in Sydney for a year. She was three months pregnant when he was offered the opportunity in Sydney, and they decided she would remain in India until after the child was born, because their visa did not give them access to affordable healthcare for the pregnancy and birth. In India, she lived, somewhat reluctantly, with her husband's parents and sister, who shared responsibility for domestic tasks and baby care. She also had access to paid domestic help. Simran's parents lived with them in Sydney for the first five months. Since they left, Simran has found the transition to sole responsibility for all domestic tasks and childcare very tiring.

Simran feels lonely. She spends most of her time alone with her toddler while her husband is at work. Recently, she met another Indian mother in the local shopping centre who told her about the Facebook group for Indian mothers in Sydney and a local Indian mothers' WhatsApp group. Simran joined both groups and now meets up with other Indian mothers during the day with their children, and sometimes in the evenings without children. She has been to dance classes and the cinema with them. She says the groups give her a chance to connect as a woman, and not just as a mother. She also has access to information about community events and festivals, and she can watch (and participate in) online conversations. Simran wishes she had found the group earlier. Bringing up a baby has been the hardest thing she has ever done, she says, harder than her MBA or anything in her working life. She looks forward to her daughter attending childcare so she can return to paid employment.

Introducing the administrators

Unlike many studies of online communities, this study attends to the experiences of the groups' creators and managers, not just their members. In the context of a site like Facebook, where it is relatively simple for users to create groups, non-specialist individuals can easily become 'accidental community managers,' responsible for, in Facebook's words, "groups that quickly become the most important part of someone's experience on Facebook" (Jin 2017). This section briefly introduces the administrators, while their role and practices are examined in more detail in Chapter 4.

The women who ran the migrant maternal online communities were all aged between 34 and 45 at time of the interview, with children ranging in age from infants to teenagers. On average, they had become mothers for the first time at the age of 31, slightly older than the national average of 29.3 (Australian Institute of Health and Welfare 2020). They all had one or two children, except for Nicole, who had three. The fifteen administrators came from India (3), Sweden (3),[17] Germany (2), Brazil (2), the United Kingdom (1), Malaysia (1), Colombia (1), Iran (1), and Singapore (1). On average, the administrators had lived in Australia for longer than the members interviewed (10 years, compared to 7 years).

Administrators cited both self-oriented and community-oriented reasons for creating the groups. That is, they were motivated by what they could obtain and what they could provide for others. Social factors predominated in both sets of reasons. *Self-oriented social reasons* included a desire for connection or friendship, a place to chat and share experiences. Secondary self-oriented reasons included a need for a support network, information, and connection to their culture. *Community-oriented reasons* revolved around creating a means for other people to chat, make connections, and find help and information. Only one administrator, Sherry, cited purely self-oriented informational goals as her motivation. Overall, social interaction appeared to be the primary aim of creating the groups, with information-sharing a secondary aim, alongside support and cultural connection. This suggests the groups might fit within an "information grounds" framework, in which information exchange is a by-product of social interaction in a space.

Karen Fisher's "information grounds" scholarship theorises information exchange as a by-product of social interaction in particular spaces, such as health clinics, playgrounds, and workplaces. People gather at these information grounds "for a primary, instrumental purpose other than information sharing" and benefit from the information they obtain "along physical, social, affective, and cognitive dimensions" (Fisher & Naumer 2006, p. 99). Information grounds research highlights how the varied types of interactions and individuals in a specific space combine to create a rich context for information-sharing. The concept of "information grounds" facilitates an understanding of the migrant maternal groups as spaces that combine information exchange, emotions, sociality, spatiality, and belonging. With its emphasis on information gathering as a by-product of interactions in everyday space, it is particularly useful for exploring "everyday life information-seeking" (Savolainen 1995).

Migrants and mothers are groups that have significant information needs and are, to varying extents, navigating unfamiliar territory. Studies indicate that migrants and mothers use a wide range of information grounds, that they value both social and informational interactions, and that these interactions support their settlement in a new place or new maternal role. As Khoir et al. (2015) note, "Information grounds are the places where immigrants meet, share with other people and get involved in social interactions. These are crucial activities during their settlement that deserve to be further explored" (p. 2). Recurrent themes in the maternal literature include the centrality of information sourced from other mothers, and the relations of sociality, support, judgement, or co-constructed maternal identity that are imbricated in an exchange of information that takes place within the "bewilderingly overdetermined discursive territory" of contemporary motherhood (Quiney 2007, p. 36).

Ana

Ana met her Australian husband in Brazil and came to settle with him in his hometown of Melbourne in 2006. Based on her previous experience of living in the UK, Ana felt nervous about moving to Australia, fearing hostility towards her as a migrant. She was also worried about leaving behind her close-knit family, her job, and culture in Brazil. Before migrating, she found a group for Brazilians in Melbourne on the social network Orkut and posted on there. The day after she arrived, six or seven people from the group came to greet her, and they became friends. A few years later, when some of them became pregnant around the same time, they decided to create the Facebook group for Brazilian mothers in Melbourne. Now 35, Ana has two young children and runs her own retail company. Having initially focused on assimilating into Australian culture, Ana feels the group has allowed her to reconnect with her Brazilian "roots" and incorporate elements of Brazilian culture into her family life. Five years after starting the group, Ana says she would feel "lost" and "unsupported" without the connections and advice provided through it. Ana takes a serious approach to her role as admin of the mothers' group, spending 10–15 hours a week on tasks relating to it. She finds it demanding but satisfying, describing herself as a "proud mum" of the group, particularly when she reflects on the support mothers receive from each other.

Reflecting on her reasons for starting the group, Ana remembers,

> We just thought, our culture in Brazil is very different from here, so when you come here and you're exposed to the culture, and you have the nurse telling you what to do, and your mum telling you the other thing completely different, because the culture is so different, all of us we felt that we were lost a bit, and it would be very good to exchange experiences between mothers, [...] to try to mix a bit of both cultures and get together as well. [...] The main thing was to get together and to exchange experiences because we found it a bit tricky, motherhood.

Information exchange as settlement strategy

This section briefly describes the main activities performed in the groups before focusing on activities involving the pursuit and provision of information. Activity levels in the groups varied, with some groups seeing many more interactions than others. For example, the Brazilian mothers' group was very active online, with questions posted and answered several times a day, and administrators took an interventionist approach to ensuring the group ran smoothly. In some groups, the interactions predominantly took place offline. For example, the Persian mothers' group saw few online interactions, with most of the meaningful activity occurring during the playgroup organised by the group's administrator. In some cases, the activities and focus had shifted over the lifetime of the group. The group for Swedish mothers in Sydney started primarily with offline meet-ups, but as the founders' children got older, and many mothers returned to work, the group's focus shifted more to online communication.

Broadly speaking, the main activities reported by participants were:

- Seeking and offering information
- Seeking and offering emotional and practical support
- Building social connections and friendships
- Organising offline events and meet-ups
- Buying and selling (mostly second-hand) goods
- Renting property and finding accommodation for visitors

This categorisation draws on the answers provided by administrators and group members during the interviews. It reflects, therefore, the relative importance placed on the various activities by the participants and the frequency with which they were reported. It is not drawn from a content analysis of posts on the group. Not all activities occurring under the auspices of the group would be available for content analysis. Activities occurring at offline events may not be referred to online. In addition, interviews revealed that reading, searching, and private messages between group members were all common activities leaving little or no trace in the semi-public space of the online discussion section.

Participants described five main ways in which information was sought and provided in the group. Firstly, members can write a post in the 'discussion' area of the group, requesting information. This post is visible to all members, who can choose whether to respond, either by writing a comment underneath the post or by contacting the poster by private message. Secondly, members can use the search function to look for previous posts on a similar topic. Thirdly, members can seek information from each other during their offline meet-ups. Fourthly, members may use the tactic described by Winnie, a Malaysian mother living in Melbourne. Rather than posting on the group, or searching previous posts, Winnie chose specific members she felt "comfortable" to approach, requested to become Facebook friends with them, and then asked them questions in a one-to-one online conversation. Finally, some participants described providing unsolicited information by posting links to articles on topics they considered of interest to their fellow group members.

Most commonly, the information sought and provided revolved around setting up family life in a new country. For example, finding schools, childcare, and doctors; buying cars; finding accommodation; navigating welfare and health systems; and so on. Mothers also sought information on where to purchase specific products they were used to buying in their country of origin; most commonly, food and ingredients. Many questions revolved around visits home: advice on flying long distances with young children, airline recommendations, accommodation, or activity ideas for the trip. Two members of a Swedish mothers' group, each flying alone with two children, arranged to fly at the same time for mutual support. Participants sought information about local children's activities; where to go to celebrate cultural festivals; advice on passports, birth registrations, citizenship issues, and international money transfers; recipes and remedies specific to their country of origin; and advice on managing postnatal depression and other mental health issues.

For some participants, the online mothers' group was their primary source of information. Simran explained, "So, anything related to myself, or for my baby. So, if I do not know, then I would ask." The types of questions sometimes reflected differences between Australia and members' countries of origin. For example, many Swedish migrant parents are surprised by the difference in childcare systems, particularly the level of fees, so this elicits frequent questions in the Swedish groups. In the Indian, Singaporean, and Malaysian groups, questions about education are common, as mothers attempt to navigate different systems and conflicting educational philosophies and techniques. Karen, the administrator of the group for Singaporean mothers in Melbourne, recalled discussions on the relative lack of homework in Australian schools and noted that members bought school workbooks on visits to Singapore and sold them to other members of the group.

In proposing information exchange as a maternal relational settlement activity (Williams Veazey 2019, p. 2), I conceptualise settlement as ongoing negotiation, rather than a short-lived transition or assimilation. Simran, a relatively new migrant with a young baby, had little access to local information before joining the Indian mothers' group and used the group to gain a sense of familiarity with local facilities and norms as part of an initial settlement process. However, Karen's experience, which is based on observations of Singaporean migrants with older children, many of whom have lived in Australia for years, suggests migrant mothers may continue to seek information from each other as they navigate unfamiliar systems such as education. Aditi imagined consulting her Indian mothers' group as her children reach school age in a few years:

> I'm quite interested in how mums with older kids perceive education. And I think when my time comes, it will be handy. Like private schooling, public schooling, there are quite strong opinions on there, so I think when my time comes, it will be interesting for how I perceive things. Things like whether to hold off your child or don't hold off.[18] With Australians, it's very common to hold off, whereas in India, it comes, you find it hard, it's difficult to accept that you're holding off your child for this reason.

Aditi's comments suggest that mothers' need for information may be intimately bound up with the phases of their children's life. Rather than fading according to time since arrival, migrant mothers' information needs may attain renewed salience as their children move through milestones, such as vaccinations, starting school, or adolescence. For migrant mothers, this pursuit of information is part of an active negotiation that considers local customs alongside the norms of their country of origin. Those norms are not consigned to the past; rather, they form an active part of discussions with family and friends, and with fellow members of these online groups.

Information-seeking in the Brazilian mothers' group

The Brazilian mothers' group sees frequent online discussions. New and prospective migrants seek advice from more settled members about which suburb to move to, how the health and education systems work, and how to find a good school or doctor. They ask for recommendations of Brazilian doctors, dentists, nannies, cleaners, masseuses, manicurists, and other service providers. Mothers commonly ask questions relating to children's food and sleep. Discussions around bullying or illnesses elicit heartfelt responses. Members share recipes and meal ideas. During the Zika virus outbreak,[19] members discussed the safety of travelling to Brazil. So much information has been shared in the group that the administrators have compiled some of it into files stored in the group, and some has even been collated in a pamphlet that is now distributed to new migrants by the local Brazilian consulate. One of the administrators, Ana, shares articles with the group about parenting, particularly children's sleep and behaviour issues, and information about migration, such as how she has supported her mother to migrate to Australia.

Information exchange as social strategy

Information grounds theory positions information as a by-product of social interaction in specific spaces and was initially developed in relation to offline spaces. Many theories of online information behaviours, however, position the pursuit of information as the primary goal, with social connections as the means or facilitator. For example, Pirolli's "social information foraging" theory (2009) posits that having access to multiple clusters of information is advantageous in enabling people to make connections between bits of information held in different places, and thus create new knowledge. His focus remains individualistic, acknowledging the benefits of group membership for providing "actual or potential resources that can be utilized or mobilized to achieve individual goals" (p. 606). Some women in the study did approach the groups in this way. For example, Sherry created the group for Malaysian mothers in preparation for her move, specifically inviting mothers who were already living in Australia, as they would be best placed to answer her questions. Similarly, when Aoife was preparing to move from Singapore to Sydney, she joined the UK/Irish mothers' group for the "shared tacit knowledge" it contained, seeking answers to questions like, "How do I set up GP registration? What vaccinations do I have to have? What stuff should I buy when I'm home in Europe for Christmas that you can't get here?"

For Pirolli, the social is a means to an individualistic end. By contrast, information grounds theory accounts for a two-way interaction between sociality and information. That is, information-sharing facilitates social interaction and vice versa. It has been suggested that in online spaces information-sharing may play a more significant social role than in offline spaces (Counts & Fisher 2010). As Pelaprat and Brown also argue:

> Posting a question or responding to a question on a forum is not an isolated social action where the goal is simply having your question answered. It is, rather, a first move of [sic] in a series of turn-taking exchanges that form social bonds of diverse kinds.
>
> (2012, para. 39)

Thus, information exchange can be both a means of seeking sociality and a by-product of social interaction. The relative importance of information or sociality for an individual may change over time in relation to life course and length of involvement in the information ground. To illustrate this, the following analysis attends in turn to the administrators' motivations for creating their group; the members' motivations for joining; and the activities performed and observed by the group members.

As discussed above, a desire for social interaction drove most administrators' decision to create their group, with information exchange an important secondary reason. For members, social reasons also dominated their reasons for joining, with most hoping to find friendship or a support network, to arrange to meet up, and to 'connect' with people. For a minority of interview participants, information-seeking was the primary motivator, predominantly information needed to effect successful family settlement (health, housing, education, and childcare) and cultural maintenance (information about festivals and procuring culturally specific food, clothes, or services). Two participants, Aoife and Jyoti, emphasised that they joined only for information-seeking, dismissing the social and affective practices they observed others undertaking. Aoife noted, "I'm certainly not a group member who necessarily wants to meet any of these people face to face or – I don't take that kind of support from them. I use them [for] information-seeking ...." For Jyoti, the Indian mothers' group is useful for finding information about "Indian things," but she does not consider them to be her "counsel" or "go-to people" for support.

For many other participants, however, sociality was their primary motivator for joining. A few hoped sociality might bring the opportunity to learn from other mothers. Simran, a recent migrant from India, cited socialising as her primary motivator but recognised the informational by-products of that socialising: "Every time I meet them, I learn something new. [...] They make you more familiar with the space." Knowledge acquisition through social interaction helps Simran feel "more familiar" with her local environment, an important step in feeling 'at home' after migration (Hage 1997).

While social practices dominated the *motivations* for creating and joining groups, an analysis of reported *uses* of the group found that information-centred practices were more commonly mentioned. Participants reported using the groups to ask and respond to questions, to exchange advice, to learn from each other, and to find information and services. This information-seeking related to both emotional topics – such as how to manage loneliness, homesickness, family relationships – and instrumental information – about systems, products, and services. Social practices such as finding friends, socialising, arranging to meet up, and chatting were mentioned but were less prominent than the informational aspects. Cultural and community factors comprised a third theme. Included in this were responses around feeling closer to home through their participation in the group, accessing cultural or linguistic opportunities for themselves or their children, arranging or discussing festivals, and accessing a sense of community. Other uses of the group included buying, selling, or borrowing goods (usually books, toys, and clothing) and discussing news and current affairs.

This contrast between interviewees' reasons for joining their group and what they reported doing once they had joined is reflected in the survey responses too. Survey respondents who had joined online groups for migrant mothers cited a desire to "connect" with people with shared experiences and/or identities and to make new friends and meet other mothers. Information-seeking was also a strong motivator but was mentioned less often than the desire for interpersonal connection. When asked what they used the groups for, however, that order was reversed. A quantitative textual analysis showed that terms like "information", "advice," "questions," "tips," and "recommendations" were cited more frequently than terms like "friends" or "friendship," "meet," "connecting," or "socialising."

The participants' aspirations for social interaction suggest the information-sharing practices they describe are part of a social strategy. As Pelaprat and Brown suggest, an initial post is an "invitation to dialogue" as much as it is a request for help, and a response to a question is also a response "to the call to recognise and be recognised" (2012, para. 36). Participants gain practical information through these exchanges and obtain the social interaction they seek. Together, these interactions affect participants' sense of community, belonging, and identity.

Conclusion

This chapter has set out the ways in which the participants, as administrators and members of the Facebook groups, come together and understand their roles in the communities as they form. Creating and joining the migrant maternal groups provides an opportunity for migrant mothers to claim, negotiate, and re-shape individual and collective identities. In a re-working of Benedict Anderson's concept of "imagined communities" (2006 [1983]), these migrant mothers deploy common sense and emotional understandings of their national, maternal, and migrant identities in search of the locally emplaced information and social connections they need to navigate their lives as migrant mothers in Australia. As part of that process, migrant mothers use the affordances of closed Facebook groups to gain access to relevant information while maintaining a sense of control over disclosures of personal information. The next chapter examines the emotional, relational, and social dimensions of migrant motherhood and explores the role of the groups in counteracting migrant maternal isolation and constructing spaces and relationships of belonging.

Notes

1 All names are pseudonyms.
2 Some of the content of this chapter has been previously published as Williams Veazey, L. (2019). All in the same boat? Migration and motherhood online, in Zufferey & Buchanan (Eds.), *Intersections of Mothering: Feminist accounts* (Routledge) and has been reproduced with permission.
3 Two of the Melbourne-based groups were created and run by the same administrators; one for the whole of Melbourne and one for the sub-metropolitan area of Melbourne where they lived.
4 This group has continued to grow and at time of writing (February 2020) has over 21,000 members.
5 In one case, the language used for the group's name acted as an implied place of origin referent. So, the group name, written in Swedish, referred to "Sydney Mothers."
6 UK/Irish; German (Sydney); Malaysian; Persian; Desi; Singaporean.
7 Swedish Sydney suburbs; Spanish-speaking; Scandinavian Melbourne.

8 Indian Sydney; Brazilian. In practice, many of the mothers' groups included women providing services such as childcare, cleaning, and tutoring. Some of them would also be mothers, of course.
9 Text last checked and correct at 7/2/2016.
10 Following the completion of data collection, however, a Facebook group for Indian fathers in Sydney was created. The group appears to be modelled on the Indian mothers' group in this study, citing the mothers' group in their public description and guidelines.
11 One exception is education research, where there is a growing body of scholarship looking at students' use of Facebook groups as learning environments (for example, Carmichael & MacEachen 2017; Sheeran & Cummings 2018). In migration research, a recent thesis explored the use of (public) Facebook groups by Italian migrants in Australia (C. Davis 2017).
12 As I write in February 2020, this Indian mothers' group now has over 20,000 members and, according to figures generated by Facebook, has seen an average of 80 posts per day over the past month.
13 28 in Australia, the others in a third country (not their home country). Includes women who were temporarily in their home country but knew they would be migrating to join their partner and/or were only temporarily at home to give birth but usually lived in another country.
14 The British-Indian interviewee (also a member of the UK/Irish group) was married to a British-Indian man she had met in Australia.
15 Again, Kavita, the British-Indian migrant, is an exception. She was very conscious of needing outside support to enable her to pass down an Indian cultural identity to her daughter successfully.
16 All figures in this paragraph are rounded for clarity.
17 Although born in Central America, Sabina identified most strongly with Sweden, the country where she was raised.
18 Aditi is referring to the choice some parents have in New South Wales about their child's school starting age.
19 In 2015, there was an outbreak of the Zika virus in Brazil. Infection in pregnant women may cause pregnancy complications and birth defects (WHO 2018).

References

Anderson, B. R. O. G. (2006). *Imagined communities: Reflections on the origin and spread of nationalism*. New York; London: Verso (Original work published 1983).
Arnold, L. B. (2011). 10 years out: Presence and absence in a long-term online mothers' community. In M. Moravec (Ed.), *Motherhood online* (pp. 73–96). Newcastle Upon Tyne: Cambridge Scholars Publishing.
Australian Bureau of Statistics. (2017). 2016 Census Quickstats. Retrieved from http://www.abs.gov.au/websitedbs/D3310114.nsf/Home/2016 QuickStats.
Australian Institute of Health and Welfare. (2020). Australia's mothers and babies 2018 – in brief. Retrieved from https://www.aihw.gov.au/reports/mothers-babies/australias-mothers-and-babies-2018-in-brief/contents/table-of-contents.
Barnes, M., Courtney, M., Pratt, J., & Walsh, A. (2003). Contemporary child health nursing practice: Services provided and challenges faced in metropolitan and outer Brisbane areas. *Collegian*, 10(4), 14–19. doi:10.1016/S1322-7696(08)60071-60072.
boyd, d. (2010). Social network sites as networked publics: Affordances, dynamics, and implications. In Z. Papacharissi (Ed.), *A networked self: Identity, community and culture on social network sites*. New York: Routledge.

Cameron, A. J., Charlton, E., Walsh, A., Hesketh, K., & Campbell, K. (2019). The influence of the maternal peer group (partner, friends, mothers' group, family) on mothers' attitudes to obesity-related behaviours of their children. *BMC Pediatrics*, 19(1), 357.

Canterbury City Community Centre. (2017). Family creative play day. Retrieved from https://www.4cs.org.au/news-events/events/family-creative-play-day.

Carmichael, D., & MacEachen, C. (2017). Heuristic evaluation of the use of Blackboard & Facebook Groups in computing higher education. *International Journal of Modern Education and Computer Science*, 9(6), 1–8. doi:10.5815/ijmecs.2017.06.01.

Chalklen, C., & Anderson, H. (2017). Mothering on Facebook: Exploring the privacy/ openness paradox. *Social Media + Society*, 3(2). doi:10.1177/2056305117707187.

Chambers, D. (2013). *Social media and personal relationships: Online intimacies and networked friendship*. Basingstoke: Palgrave Macmillan.

Chambers, D. (2017). Networked intimacy: Algorithmic friendship and scalable sociality. *European Journal of Communication*, 32(1), 26–36. doi:10.1177/0267323116682792.

Commerford, J., & Robinson, E. (2016). *Supported playgroups for parents and children: The evidence for their benefits*. Melbourne, Australia: Australian Institute of Family Studies. Retrieved from https://aifs.gov.au/cfca/publications/supported-playgroups-pa rents-and-children/introduction.

Counts, S., & Fisher, K. E. (2010). Mobile social networking as information ground: A case study. *Library and Information Science Research*, 32(2), 98–115. doi:10.1016/j. lisr.2009.10.003.

Davis, C. (2017). Managing and imagining migration: The role of Facebook groups in the lives of "new" Italian migrants in Australia. (Dissertation/Thesis). The University of Sydney. Retrieved from http://hdl.handle.net/2123/17346.

Davis, J. L., & Jurgenson, N. (2014). Context collapse: Theorizing context collusions and collisions. *Information, Communication & Society*, 17(4), 476–485. doi:10.1080/ 1369118X.2014.888458.

Davis, K. E. (2015). The information experience of new mothers in social media: A grounded theory study. (PhD). Retrieved from http://eprints.qut.edu.au/86784/.

Drentea, P., & Moren-Cross, J. L. (2005). Social capital and social support on the web: The case of an internet mother site. *Sociology of Health & Illness*, 27(7), 920–943. doi:10.1111/j.1467-9566.2005.00464.x.

Drentea, P., & Moren-Cross, J. L. (2011). Online motherhood: A community of mothers revisited. In M. Moravec (Ed.), *Motherhood online* (pp. 45–59). Newcastle Upon Tyne: Cambridge Scholars Publishing.

Dunham, P. J., Hurshman, A., Litwin, E., Gusella, J., Ellsworth, C., & Dodd, P. W. D. (1998). Computer-mediated social support: Single young mothers as a model system. *American Journal of Community Psychology*, 26(2), 281–306. doi:10.1023/ A:1022132720104.

Ellison, N. B., Vitak, J., Steinfield, C., Gray, R., & Lampe, C. (2011). Negotiating privacy concerns and social capital needs in a social media environment. In S. Trepte, & L. Reinecke (Eds.), *Privacy online: Perspectives on privacy and self-disclosure in the social web* (pp. 19–32). Berlin, Heidelberg: Springer.

Fisher, K. E., & Naumer, C. M. (2006). Information grounds: Theoretical basis and empirical findings on information flow in social settings. In A. Spink, & C. Cole (Eds.), *New directions in human information behavior* (pp. 93–111). Springer.

Gibson, L., & Hanson, V. L. (2013). *'Digital motherhood' Chi '13 proceedings of the SIGCHI conference on human factors in computing systems* (pp. 313–322). New York: Association for Computing Machinery.

Gregory, T., Harman-Smith, Y., Sincovich, A., Wilson, A., & Brinkman, S. (2016). *It takes a village to raise a child: The influence and impact of playgroups across Australia*. Retrieved from https://playgroupaustralia.org.au/resource/it-takes-a-village-to-raise-a-child/.

Hage, G. (1997). At home in the entrails of the west. In H. Grace, G. Hage, L. Johnson, J. Langsworth, & M. Symonds (Eds.), *Home/world: Space, community and marginality in Sydney's west* (pp. 99–153). Annandale, NSW: Pluto Press.

Hicks, M. (2010). New groups: Stay closer to groups of people in your life. Retrieved from https://www.facebook.com/notes/facebook/new-groups-stay-closer-to-groups-of-people-in-your-life/434700832130.

Inner West Mums [Facebook group]. (2018). Retrieved from https://www.facebook.com/groups/InnerWestMums1.

Jensen, T. (2013). Mumsnetiquette: Online affect within parenting culture. In C. Maxwell, & P. Aggleton (Eds.), *Privilege, agency and affect* (pp. 127–145). Palgrave Macmillan.

Jesuit Refugee Service Australia. (2015). Arrupe place welcomes asylum seekers. Retrieved from http://www.jrs.org.au/arrupe-place-welcomes-asylum-seekers/.

Jin, K.-X. (2017). Our first communities summit and new tools for group admins. Retrieved from https://newsroom.fb.com/news/2017/06/our-first-communities-summit-and-new-tools-for-group-admins/.

Johnson, S. (2015). 'Intimate mothering publics': Comparing face-to-face support groups and internet use for women seeking information and advice in the transition to first-time motherhood. *Culture, Health & Sexuality*, 17(2), 237–251. doi:10.1080/13691058.2014.968807.

Khoir, S., Du, J. T., & Koronios, A. (2015). Everyday information behaviour of Asian immigrants in South Australia: A mixed-methods exploration. *Information Research*, 20(3).

Kim, J., Ahn, J., & Vitak, J. (2015). Korean mothers' kakaostory use and its relationship to psychological well-being. *First Monday*, 20(3).

Lawson, J. S., & Callaghan, A. (1991). Recreating the village: The development of groups to improve social relationships among mothers of newborn infants in Australia. *Australian Journal of Public Health*, 15(1), 64–66. doi:10.1111/j.1753-6405.1991.tb00012.x.

Madge, C., & O'Connor, H. (2004). 'My mum's thirty years out of date'. *Community, Work & Family*, 7(3), 351–369. doi:10.1080/1366880042000295754.

Madge, C., & O'Connor, H. (2005). Mothers in the making? Exploring liminality in cyber/space. *Transactions of the Institute of British Geographers*, 30(1), 83–97. doi:10.1111/j.1475-5661.2005.00153.x.

Madge, C., & O'Connor, H. (2006). Parenting gone wired: Empowerment of new mothers on the internet? *Social & Cultural Geography*, 7(2), 199–220. doi:10.1080/14649360600600528.

Marwick, A. E., & boyd, d. (2011). I tweet honestly, I tweet passionately: Twitter users, context collapse, and the imagined audience. *New Media & Society*, 13(1), 114–133. doi:10.1177/1461444810365313.

Nicastri, D. (2014, 27/08/2014). North Shore Mums Facebook group put on Bollywood extravaganza at Urban Tadka Indian restaurant in Terrey Hills. *North Shore Times*. Retrieved from https://www.dailytelegraph.com.au/newslocal/north-shore/

north-shore-mums-facebook-group-put-on-bollywood-extravaganza-at-urban-tadka
-indian-restaurant-in-terrey-hills/news-story/6240859204dd73188044edc2a8d22313.

North Shore Mums (Sydney) [Facebook group]. (2018). Retrieved from https://www.fa cebook.com/groups/northshoremums/.

NSW Health. (2010). Maternal & child health primary health care policy (PD2010_017). Retrieved from http://www1.health.nsw.gov.au/pds/ActivePDSDo cuments/PD2010_017.pdf.

Pedersen, S., & Lupton, D. (2018). 'What are you feeling right now?' Communities of maternal feeling on Mumsnet. *Emotion, Space and Society*, 26, 57–63. doi:10.1016/j. emospa.2016.05.001.

Pelaprat, E., & Brown, B. (2012). Reciprocity: Understanding online social relations. *First Monday*, 17(10). doi:10.5210/fm.v17i10.3324.

Pettigrew, K. E. (1999). Waiting for chiropody: Contextual results from an ethnographic study of the information behaviour among attendees at community clinics. *Information Processing and Management*, 35(6), 801–817. doi:10.1016/S0306-4573(99)00027-8.

Pirolli, P. (2009). *An elementary social information foraging model*. Paper presented at the Proceedings of the SIGCHI Conference on Human Factors in Computing Systems.

Playgroup NSW. (2017). Playgroups for refugee families. Retrieved from http://www. playgroupnsw.org.au/News/PlaygroupStories/playgroups-for-refugee-families.

Quiney, R. (2007). Confessions of the new capitalist mother: Twenty-first-century writing on motherhood as trauma. *Women: A Cultural Review*, 18(1), 19–40. doi:10.1080/09574040701276704.

Savolainen, R. (1995). Everyday life information seeking: Approaching information seeking in the context of "way of life". *Library and Information Science Research*, 17(3), 259–294. doi:10.1016/0740-8188(95)90048-9.

Scott, D., Brady, S., & Glynn, P. (2001). New mother groups as a social network intervention: Consumer and maternal and child health nurse perspectives. *The Australian Journal of Advanced Nursing*, 18(4), 23–29.

Settlement Services International. (2017). Multicultural playgroup helps newly arrived social worker regain her confidence. Retrieved from https://www.ssi.org.au/news/ssi- news-blog/1117-multicultural-playgroup-helps-newly-arrived-social-worker-regain-her- confidence.

Sheeran, N., & Cummings, D. J. (2018). An examination of the relationship between Facebook groups attached to university courses and student engagement. *Higher Education*, 76(6), 937–955. doi:10.1007/s10734-018-0253-2.

Strange, C., Fisher, C., Howat, P., & Wood, L. (2014). Fostering supportive community connections through mothers' groups and playgroups. *Journal of Advanced Nursing*, 70(12), 2835–2846. doi:10.1111/jan.12435.

VICSEG New Futures. (2014). Playgroups for diverse communities. Retrieved from http:// www.communityhubs.org.au/wp-content/uploads/2017/10/VICSEG_Evidence_into_Act on_paper_-_Playgroups_for_Diverse_Communities_Sep_14.pdf.

Walther, K. (2014). In defence of our mothers' community: The other side of the story. Retrieved from https://www.mamamia.com.au/north-shore-mums/.

Warr, D., Mann, R., Forbes, D., & Turner, C. (2013). Once you've built some trust: Using playgroups to promote children's health and wellbeing for families from migrant backgrounds. *Australasian Journal of Early Childhood*, 38(1), 41–48.

Williams Veazey, L. (2019). Glocalised motherhood: Sociality and affect in migrant mothers' online communities. *Feminist Encounters: A Journal of Critical Studies in Culture and Politics*, 3(1–2), 09. doi:10.20897/femenc/5915.

World Health Organization. (2018). Zika virus. Retrieved from https://www.who.int/en/news-room/fact-sheets/detail/zika-virus.

3 Migrant mothers' relational, affective, and social settlement practices

Introduction

Siobhan

I meet Siobhan, a 40-year-old Irish migrant, in her apartment in central Sydney. It is a quiet block, where few other families live. All the mothers' groups and baby clinics take place at least a bus ride away, which she has found difficult with a newborn baby. Even her nurse refused to visit her when she left the hospital, as there was nowhere for her to park near the apartment. Siobhan's husband got a new job shortly before their son was born, working longer hours, sometimes six or seven days a week. As relatively new migrants and soon-to-be parents, they felt he had to take the work that was offered, whatever the impact on their family life.

Back home in Ireland, she lived close to her parents and saw her mother nearly every day. Her mother looks after her other grandchildren until they go to school, and her mother's house is the "meeting point" for the whole family. Living in the same town she'd grown up in, Siobhan had a large network of friends and family. Her husband's family also lived nearby. The contrast is stark with the long days she now spends alone with her baby. She imagines the companionship of having friends or family to bring her a cup of tea, or hold the baby for a moment, and the freedom of taking the baby "out for a spin" in the car, none of which she experiences in Sydney.

For Siobhan, loneliness has been the most challenging aspect of her migration experience, even before becoming a mother. Neither antenatal classes nor her council-supported mothers' group have resulted in ongoing friendships. At the time of the interview, she looked forward to returning to work, where she had made friends before she went on maternity leave. It was her (Australian) manager who told her about the UK/Irish mothers' group. Although she has never met up with anyone from the group, she finds it reassuring to know that she could. She joined when she was pregnant and was comforted to see that women still socialised once they became mothers. Observing interactions in the group reassures Siobhan that she is "not the only person feeling that way"– that is, lonely and homesick.

Migration[1] has often been considered from the perspective of economic and political rationality. Recent scholarship has emphasised the importance of applying an emotional lens to migration (Alinejad & Ponzanesi 2020; Boccagni & Baldassar 2015; Wilding et al. 2020). Building on this scholarship, this chapter explores migration as a social and emotional experience and draws attention to the ways in which migrant mothers use migrant maternal online communities to help them navigate a path through the emotional and social challenges of migrant motherhood. Key themes include isolation, friendship, failure, homesickness, guilt, and disconnection. Chapter 4 includes a discussion on the "emotional practices" (Bareither 2019) enacted in the groups and explores how the groups' administrators seek to curate the emotional environment of their group. In this chapter, I focus on how difficult emotions can be perceived as a barrier to feeling 'at home' in a new country and how online social relations enable migrant mothers to explain and explore their emotions and reconcile them with the possibility of a new sense of belonging.

Online connectivity allows contemporary migrants to maintain social relations across time and space, sustaining caring, affective, and social relationships with people to whom they are no longer proximate (Diminescu 2008; Kędra 2020; Wilding 2006). Nevertheless, new migrants (and new mothers) also need to create new social relationships (Gibson & Hanson 2013; Gilmartin & Migge 2016; Westcott & Vazquez Maggio 2016). Indeed, I argue, these new social relationships are a core means by which migrant mothers make a place for themselves in their new environment. As we have seen in Chapter 2, these new relationships can be formed in face-to-face mothers' groups, in playgroups, and in the school playground (Gilmartin & Migge 2016). In present day Australia, online groups run by and for migrant mothers are another means by which migrant mothers seek to rebuild their social infrastructure, which has been disrupted by migration and/or motherhood.

While research exists on maternal isolation and, to a lesser extent, on migrant maternal isolation, the issues of friendship, sociality, and relational belonging in migrant motherhood remain relatively unexplored. This chapter investigates how migrant mothers become an affective resource for each other, thereby counteracting widespread isolation and constructing spaces and relationships of belonging. Highlighting migrant mothers' agency, this chapter analyses the ways they respond to isolation and ruptures in their social infrastructure, exploring some of the strategies they deploy to construct new forms of belonging and community.

Central to this exploration is the concept of "relational settlement." Diminescu coined this phrase to describe how connections to people in the destination country facilitate certain migration decisions (2008, pp. 570–572). This definition of "relational settlement" foregrounds the facilitation of mobility. Bringing this concept into conversation with Gedalof's (2009) call for a deeper analysis of the "reproductive" processes of creating material and emotional stability in migrant contexts, I have used the phrase "relational settlement" to describe how migrants build a sense of *belonging* through the establishment of *new* social networks and relationships (Williams Veazey 2019, p. 2; Williams Veazey forthcoming). Used in this way, "relational settlement" refers to relational processes and practices that have a "home-building" sensibility (Hage 1997). Relationships are salient across distance *and* in proximity; for mobility *and* "inhabitance" (Gedalof 2009; see also Ebaugh & Curry 2000). As Gedalof (2009) argues, a relational approach highlights the importance of "nearness, inter-dependency and the construction of bonds between selves" in a migrant context (p. 93) and brings to light the often overlooked work performed by mothers to achieve stability and belonging for them and their family.

As important as relational settlement is the concept of affective settlement. On a descriptive level, affective settlement refers to the salience of emotions in the process of migration and, more specifically, in the process of building a sense of home and belonging in a new place (Hage 1997). On an analytical level, affective settlement refers to the role of the emotions in facilitating or inhibiting those processes. This chapter moves between those two registers, describing the experiences of migrant mothers in terms of loneliness and friendship, homesickness and belonging, guilt and love, and also how migrant mothers utilise these shared emotional experiences to build relationships of "horizontal care" (Francisco-Menchavez 2018) and a sense of belonging for themselves and their family (Gedalof 2009). One of the key roles of the online communities built by the migrant mothers is to act as a social and emotional safety net, particularly during the precarious periods of new migranthood and/or new motherhood.

Relational and affective settlement are deeply intertwined: affective settlement is made possible by developing connections with other migrant mothers, who can provide relief, validation, empathy, comfort, and reassurance. Emotions such as failure, homesickness, guilt, disconnection, and insecurity worked against participants' ability to feel 'at home' in Australia. Participating in migrant maternal communities helped participants not to overcome these emotions but to reconcile them with the possibility of belonging. I trace how this emotional home-building process works through the exchange of emotional responses between migrant mothers. Using the key themes of failure, homesickness, guilt, and disconnection, which were identified by participants as emotions that troubled their affective settlement, this chapter explores how the migrant maternal groups offer relief, validation, empathy, and comfort. In this way, the groups enable the women to build a sense of belonging in which their previously troubling emotions become sites of commonality and connection.

Scholars disagree about whether online communication is fundamentally "conducive to sociality" (Chambers 2013, p. 16) or offers "the illusion of companionship without the demands of friendship" (Turkle 2011, p. 1), manifesting in a lack of authentic intimacy and a decline in empathy (Turkle 2016). In a sense, Turkle challenges us to consider whether online communication carries any meaningful affective weight or is simply an affectively empty performance of connection (2011, p. 19). The work by Döveling et al. (2018) on "digital affect cultures" has argued that feelings such as loss, grief, connection, and belonging are not just expressed but also co-constructed in social spaces online. This chapter considers the emotional dimensions of migrant motherhood and how migrant mothers construct and navigate different levels of intimacy through the interface of the communal experience of an online group.

Isolation

Scholarly research and popular writing have investigated the close association of motherhood with loneliness and isolation (Baraitser 2009; Johnson 2017; Lee et al. 2017; McLaren 2018; Rogan et al. 1997). Numerous research reports into maternal mental health recommend increased social support to reduce isolation and increase practical support and thereby improve mental health (Balaji et al. 2007; Barclay & Kent 1998; Hetherington et al. 2018; Leahy-Warren et al. 2012). Rogan et al.'s (1997) grounded theory study of early motherhood in Australia identified "aloneness" as one of six main categories that made up the social process of "becoming a mother." More recently, findings from the Longitudinal Study of Australian children indicate that one in four mothers has nobody to confide in most of the time and less than weekly contact with friends (Australian Institute of Family Studies 2009, p. 14). Studies suggest that when migration intersects with motherhood, isolation and loneliness may be even more prominent and problematic. A 2014 meta-synthesis of recent qualitative research relating to migrant mothers' experiences of childbearing and motherhood found that "feelings of isolation, loneliness and depression from lack of support" were common across many of the studies (Benza & Liamputtong 2014, p. 582). New motherhood is a time when women require support to help them recover from birth, care for the baby, and re-shape their life (Seefat-van Teeffelen et al. 2011; Wilkins 2006). Migrant mothers often lack this support and may feel additional sadness when imagining the kind of help from family and friends they would have received 'at home' (Ward 2004, p. 80). Migrant mothers may also face barriers in seeking support, such as language barriers, difficulties navigating unfamiliar systems, fear of being judged a 'bad' mother (Ahmed et al. 2008; Schmied et al. 2017), and lack of cultural competence from service providers (DeSouza 2013). A 2010 study found that proficiency in English significantly affected whether new migrant mothers in Australia reported feelings of loneliness (Bandyopadhyay et al. 2010, p. 419). Women from non-English-speaking backgrounds may be less likely to access council-supported mothers' groups (Scott et al. 2001) and playgroups (Gregory et al. 2016) in Australia.

Motherhood and isolation are not inherently bound together, however. The association of motherhood with isolation is historically and culturally specific, and most research in this area has been undertaken in the normative context of white, middle-class mothers in nuclear family arrangements. As Adrienne Rich notes in *Of Woman Born*, mothers in pre-nineteenth century North America were rarely home alone with only children to care for, as the home was a site of intense (economic) activity, and families were large (Rich 1976). In the late twentieth century, bell hooks (1984) and Patricia Hill Collins (1991) described widespread community child-rearing in African-American communities, where neighbours and extended family provided daily childcare as well as longer-term informal adoptions and child-focused community activism. In many Australian Aboriginal communities, extended kinship families play an essential role in child-rearing, both because of enduring cultural practices and the ongoing effects of government policies that have disrupted family structures and parent–child relationships (Moore & Riley 2010). Some participants in this study came from countries in which dense networks of support in the perinatal period, extended family structures, and more collective modes of mothering were more commonplace. Nevertheless, research suggests that maternal isolation still exists even in these contexts and may be considered a risk factor for maternal and infant health (Raman et al. 2014).

Bell and Ribbens (1994) have distinguished between a "psychological sense of isolation" and "social isolation in […] localised daily life" of mothers with young children (p. 238). Their ethnographic studies, mainly with white women in South East England, highlight the significance of the "complex maternal worlds" and "webs of relationships" constructed by mothers, mostly in their local area. They argue that a dichotomous understanding around [work = public] and [home = private] has led to an under-theorisation of the social contacts and interactions of mothers that cut across private spaces (homes) and public spaces such as community groups, schools, shops, playgroups, streets, and shops. Nevertheless, they note that for many women "involvement in these networks did not develop until babies were several months old," and the time before that was "described as lonely and difficult by many women" (p. 251). Migrant mothers, whose experiences were not explored by Bell and Ribbens, may additionally experience a sense of cultural isolation or dislocation as a result of embarking on motherhood in an unfamiliar context.

In the decades since the studies conducted by Bell and Ribbens, widespread digital connectivity has facilitated the construction of "complex maternal worlds" and "webs of relationships" (p. 248) in online settings during pregnancy and the early days of motherhood, when women may not yet have developed other maternal relationships. These online connections have the potential to disrupt the [work = public = male], [home = private = female] dichotomy outlined by Bell and Ribbens. Mothers interact in the semi-public space of online groups while remaining physically in their home. They may also interact in one semi-public space (the online group) while physically present in another public or semi-public space, such as the workplace, playground, or waiting room. Participating in a locally based maternal group increases the chances of repeated interactions with the same people as opposed to relying on crossing paths in the local streets, shops, and playgrounds. For people with few local attachments, such as new migrants, those connections can provide a pathway out of isolation. Unlike the local maternal networks studied by Bell and Ribbens (1994, p. 248), the online groups do not exclude those in full-time employment as they are accessible outside work hours, or even during work hours from a smartphone, for example.

For the women in this study, experiences of isolation resulted from an intersection of factors, including motherhood, migration, work, and identity. The different ways these elements intersected in the assemblage of the participants' experiences affected how that isolation had been produced. For example, where migration coincided with, or followed shortly after, a period of maternity leave from their full-time job, the result was often an extended period as a stay-at-home mother in a new country. Sunita, who migrated from India during her first maternity leave, had hoped to find a new role in Australia with the company she had worked for before migration and maternity leave, but that did not materialise. Instead, she remained 'at home' with her son and then had a second child. Although she described the additional time with her children as a "blessing," Sunita found her unfamiliar "homemaker" role challenging without the support of the full-time nanny and other domestic help she had had in India, and she planned to look for new employment before her baby turned one. The transition away from full-time employment was not always an unwelcome change. Usha cited the desire for part-time employment and more time with her son as a motivating factor behind their migration from India. Nevertheless, the simultaneous loss of a working identity, work-related networks, and place-based networks created a strong sense of isolation, of having been "cut adrift from the social moorings secured by affective ties of family and friends, as well as community and place" (Yeoh & Khoo 1998, p. 172). Migrant mothers also experienced the loss of the "social moorings" provided by work outside the home. Where migration preceded motherhood, women's post-migration social networks often centred on the workplace, but those work-based relationships proved insufficient once women stepped outside the workplace as new mothers.

Where women had experienced the co-presence of family and paid domestic workers, their post-migration domestic responsibilities provided a stark contrast. Karen had given up her career in Singapore to move to Australia, where she became "for about three, four years, full-time mum." The sudden evaporation of both family and live-in "domestic helper" sharply increased both her domestic workload and social isolation:

> In Singapore, I have a domestic helper, who lives in with us, and I have my mum who comes every day to help out with the children, then the chores, so I don't have to do much cooking, or any housework. When I came here, everything I had to do on my own.

In Singapore, Karen's workplace and home were both spaces of social interaction. In Melbourne, life revolved around a home populated only by the members of her nuclear family.

Some women contrasted their isolated situation with the support and social contact they imagined they would have had in their home country. Even women who came from countries with similar individualised and intensive modes of mothering to those encountered in Australia imagined an alternative context with childcare and friendships on tap. For example, Lisa, Siobhan, and Gemma cited siblings 'back home' in the UK and Ireland who benefited from free childcare from their mothers. Social media highlighted these comparisons. "I see, on Facebook, my friends back home, and they're having weekends away and nights out ...," Gemma explained, noting that this socialising and respite was made possible by grandparental childcare. Some women admitted that the supportive context they imagined might not correspond with reality, their imagination glossing over the practical realities of busy lives, distances, economic realities, and family dynamics when viewed from a distance. Kavita admitted she had "rose-tinted glasses" when thinking about friends and family at home, noting "we see them more when we go back than they see of each other, and they live quite close [to each other]."

Friendship

Even in an age of digital connection, migration disrupts an individual's social infrastructure, consisting of friends, extended family, professional networks and colleagues, domestic employees, and casual acquaintances. Westcott and Vazquez Maggio (2016) argue that migration literature tends to overlook the "hidden emotional cost" of migration that results from migrants' need to make new friends. The process of initiating new friendships can be challenging, they argue, and can "contribute to the migrant's overall feelings of success and security living in a new place" (p. 505). As well as needing the instrumental support and information that friendships can bring, "the migrant faces certain loneliness unless they are able to forge social connections" (p. 505). In their study of migrant mothers in Ireland, Gilmartin and Migge (2016) noted that new friendships were a key mechanism by which their participants developed "a connection to Ireland and [...] a sense of place-belongingness" (p. 151). The study also found that participants relied on friendships with other migrant mothers because of their mutual openness to new friendships in the absence of an established network and their mutual need for support (for example, help with picking up children from school) in the absence of family support (p. 151–152). The formation of friendships is a key element of "relational settlement" but has largely been overlooked in studies of migrant motherhood.

The difficulty of establishing friendships was a prominent theme in participants' recollections, and the struggle led to loneliness, depression, low confidence, frustration, and homesickness. Winnie recalled the loneliness of her first years in Australia:

I had no friends, no one. I was pretty depressed, and I feel like I'm very separate from the society. I couldn't get into the society here, I couldn't find anybody to talk to, to understand me, to be my friend, and I had pretty low self-esteem at the time.

Participants noted the loneliness that resulted from leaving friends "back home" (Pooja), particularly friends with a shared "history" with whom they could be "brutally honest" (Michelle). Members of the German mothers' group noted that people in their area of Sydney were particularly "cliquey" (Katja), attributing this to the fact that many local people had grown up in the locality, and therefore had dense, settled social networks. Other barriers included navigating differences in modes of conversation and sociality. As Katja remarked, "Australians are easy to meet but hard to get to know." Nicole expressed frustration at the superficiality of everyday conversations, which she contrasted with Germans' more straightforward, open mode of conversation. Michelle found local mothers to be "really rude" and felt her age created an additional barrier to making friends with younger mothers. Winnie, quoted above, was a migrant from Malaysia and cited barriers created by dominant Australian cultural practices of sociality, such as alcohol-related socialising and conversations centred on sport, which she found uninteresting and alienating. Winnie was the only participant to cite racism as a factor, but other women mentioned a lack of interest among local mothers in getting to know outsiders (Nicole), or the tendency of local Australian mothers to stick together to the exclusion of migrants or non-Anglophones (Kate). Tanja recalled feeling "quite alone" when she arrived, speaking limited English, before she met another German mother through her daughter's school.

Migration is not always a one-off journey followed by permanent settlement. Participants recounted experiences of friends returning home, or moving elsewhere, their hard-earned friendships disrupted again by migration. The German mother who helped Tanja soon returned to Germany. Grainne described the emotional turmoil of seeing her friendship group "dwindle":

It's a real struggle. So, we had one big group dwindle quite rapidly about two years ago, and it was [after] they all had their second child. But in the last year or 18 months, it's been … even ones that have just had their first baby and they're going. Like my friend […] she's pregnant with her second, and there's seven weeks between her little boy and my little boy, and now there's only 12 days between our due date this time. She's going home to Ireland to have her baby. And she couldn't tell me face to face because she knew … I was devastated. Because […] we used to go to those groups together when we were on maternity leave, and she really helped me through all the struggles at the beginning and vice versa […].

Grainne associates her friends' migration decisions with their maternal journeys, a factor often overlooked in migration literature. Lisa, who moved to an outer city suburb after the birth of her second child, described how her friends are "all scattered around" as they have sought "a bigger house and more comfortable rent, as families have grown." Stefanie described a series of departures, including her sister, a German friend, and an English friend, which left her "devastated" and "upset." Assumptions about mobility can inhibit friendships before they have even begun: Michelle recalled being asked by Australians and fellow migrants how long she would be staying, indicating their unwillingness to invest in a friendship if her stay might be short-lived.

The preceding discussion demonstrates a range of issues facing migrants as they attempt to meet their need for friendship in a new country. Struggling with emotions relating to leaving friends 'back home' (Westcott 2014), migrants encounter barriers to building new friendships, including perceived unwillingness by local people to reciprocate moves towards friendship, cultural differences, language barriers, and ongoing mobility that continues to disrupt friendships. Digital connectivity enables migrants to stay in touch more easily with friends and family back home but does not erase the potential for mobility to disrupt friendships and may even enhance the sense of separation from supportive networks, engendering "that tinge of jealousy every time you FaceTime and everyone's there" (Gemma). Friendship, migration, and motherhood are closely associated in migrants' accounts. These factors help to explain the need for groups like the online migrant maternal communities where migrant mothers can befriend each other. Migrants in these settings match each other's need for friendship and can sidestep the "frustration, shame, embarrassment and alienation" that can result from failed communication with potential friends (Westcott & Vazquez Maggio 2016, p. 509).

Homesickness

Homesickness, "the distress or impairment caused by an actual or anticipated separation from home" (Thurber & Walton 2012), is often perceived in the literature as a temporary, transitional state that diminishes as one adjusts or adapts to the new context (English et al. 2017; Stroebe et al. 2015). It has also been suggested that women may experience homesickness more than men, or may be more open to discussing it and seeking support (Scharp et al. 2016). The premise of homesickness as a short-lived transitional emotion may be related to the predominance of studies with university students leaving home for the first time (English et al. 2017; Thurber & Walton 2012). By contrast, Stroebe et al. (2016) have described homesickness as a "mini-grief," suggesting a more complex phenomenon with parallels to bereavement-related grief. Drawing on the experiences of the migrant mothers in this study, their homesickness does not appear to be a temporally linear experience, with intense emotion fading gently over time. Indeed, some newer migrants had found it disconcerting to realise, from discussions on the groups, that homesickness might not diminish. Siobhan found it "kind of scary" to realise that homesickness might be a salient experience, even many years later, "because you think, oh, sure in six years' time I'll be well settled, you know, surely I won't still be thinking I want to go home!" Diya spoke dismissively of women who still participated in the British mothers' group despite having been in Australia for many years: "I just think if you've been here eighteen years, surely you've built a network for yourself." Heike declared that she had "never really had too much problems with homesickness," but for others, like Susie and Rebecca, homesickness had been a constant affective accompaniment to their lives since migration. Rebecca cited homesickness as her biggest challenge, noting: "there isn't a day that goes by where I don't wish that we were all still living in London." Susie sought counselling over many years for mental health issues relating to homesickness and spoke about how she tried to manage her feelings for the sake of her children:

> I still go off and see someone, just because you know, it still rehashes, you go through these phases of homesickness and regret and 'what have I done?' [...] And then I think, no, I've got to be strong for my kids now, because I don't want them to have a mum that's depressed and regretful and thinks 'what have I done with my life?'

Rather than fading gradually, some women's experiences of homesickness had fluctuated through significant life experiences, particularly in relation to motherhood. Stefanie recalled crying on her wedding day, otherwise a happy occasion, with the realisation that it also represented a commitment to living in Australia. Since the birth of her son, she explained, "I'm not as homesick anymore. I'm homesick, yes, for him, because I would love him to know his family a lot more." For Aoife, the most intense homesickness came when her mother returned home at the end of a month-long stay following the birth of her child:

> It's so much easier if your mum's there; you can chat and have a cup of tea, [...] I think I felt very lonely at that point, and thinking, I really wish I was at home.

The birth of Katrin's second child brought her most severe bout of homesickness. She remembered struggling to manage with two children, yearning for her mother's support: "I love my dad, but I know mum would just come and chip in."

In addition to weddings and childbirth, participants noted annual events and seasons precipitated more severe homesickness. For example, Swedish, German, and British migrants noted Christmas brought intense homesickness. Annika wistfully recalled her German childhood traditions of attending church, advent calendars, anticipation around gifts, Christmas trees, cold weather, and elaborate meals, mostly orchestrated by her mother, and contrasted that with the "laissez-faire" attitude of her in-laws: "you know, just throw something on the barbie!" This homesickness for community traditions drove some women to seek sociality with their fellow migrants. Homesickness relating to her daughter's first Diwali sent Kavita searching for the Indian mothers' group. For Eva, events organised by the Swedish Church provided a comforting link to home at Christmas time. Ana noted that a Brazilian mother had used her group to organise a Christmas dinner for other families to counteract their seasonal homesickness. Rebecca, the creator of the group for UK/Irish mothers in Sydney, explained how the group had supported her through bouts of intense homesickness, while her husband understood neither her homesickness nor the impact of the group:

> At first, I don't actually think he could understand why I was setting the group up (almost like he didn't think I needed any support). Then he seemed to feel a bit threatened by it and felt like it was a place where everyone whinged about Australia or living here!

Once again, women often found people in their intimate circles unable to provide the empathy or support they required and turned to the "horizontal care" of other migrant mothers instead (Francisco-Menchavez 2018).

Guilt

Guilt has featured prominently in scholarship on the emotional dimensions of migration (Baldassar 2015; De Silva 2017; Vermot 2015), often focusing on feelings of self-reproach relating to an inability to perform expected roles or duties, e.g. caregiving. In line with this scholarship, guilt was a key theme in these participants' narratives of migration. Whether their partner was also a migrant or Australian, women recounted a sense of migration-related guilt not entirely shared by their partner. Their guilt related specifically to depriving their children of extended family relationships, depriving their parents of a close relationship with their grandchildren, being far away and unable to carry out family responsibilities such as providing care for sick or elderly relatives, or having not spent time with relatives before they died. Kavita described herself as "completely wracked with guilt" during her first six years in Australia, a guilt which returned and redoubled once she had a child. Susie described herself as "ridden with guilt" and noted her mother had "drilled" that guilt into her, asking her, "'How could you leave us? How could you leave your family?'"

Women also expressed a sense of pre-emptive guilt about family emergencies or bereavements that had not yet occurred. Grainne explained her feelings of guilt in relation to their parents, and her sister-in-law, foreseeing future health issues which "play on our mind." Her mother-in-law had breast cancer the previous year, and Grainne stated that "if anything like that happened again, we probably would just go." Although Grainne used "we" and "our", implying that her husband shared the feelings of guilt and worry, a few minutes later she differentiated their responses: "I think with [husband]'s mother, when she had the health scare, terrible thing to say, but I think if it was my mum, I'd have gone. I think I'd be gone." Kavita, too, recalled a health scare involving her husband's parent and imagined herself acting differently:

If it had been me, and if it had been my parents, once I found out that there was a malignancy in the biopsy, I probably would have just dropped everything and gone straight home. But boys are quite different.

Participants' gendered guilt resonates with research in this area. Although Wilding (2006) has suggested that online technologies have helped overcome some of the gender divide in transnational family matters – because men's increasing involvement via email relieves some of the "kinwork" traditionally done by women (p. 135) – research suggests that female migrants still feel more responsibility for transnational caregiving, particularly when it requires in-person or emotional care, and that migration-related guilt may be gendered (Baldassar 2015; De Silva 2017; Vermot 2015). Migrant women's guilt, Baldassar suggests, is "a ubiquitous and ever-present feeling of not having adequately met kinship obligations to care" (p. 87). In Baldassar's study, Italian daughters who migrated for love or career, not economic necessity, received more parental disapproval and subsequently experienced more guilt for leaving. In De Silva's study, Sri Lankan parents expressed disappointment in their migrant sons' unwillingness to provide transnational emotional care, whereas their daughters' "constant emotion work provided satisfaction and happiness" (p. 13). In this study, guilt also related to disrupting the family network, in particular the relationships between grandparents and their grandchildren. Migration made it impossible for them to fulfil their familial role of facilitating these intergenerational relationships. In the context of gendered migration-related guilt, migrant mothers were unable to find empathy from their spouses, who, in most cases, did not experience the same intensity of guilt. In response, they sought empathy from other mothers in the same position.

Failure

Participants described the emotional challenges they faced as migrant mothers, such as loneliness, emotional isolation, guilt, homesickness, and difficulties adjusting to changed circumstances. In the context of migrant isolation and individualised maternal responsibility (see, e.g., Miller 2005), some women had attributed these challenges to a personal failure or inability to cope. The emotional isolation this engendered was enhanced by the sense that people in their intimate circles (for example, their husband, their husband's family, and non-migrant friends) did not understand, or validate, the challenges they faced. Finding others who shared their experiences enabled them to recognise the structural or contextual factors contributing to their troubles, which relieved their sense of personal failure.

Winnie, who migrated from Malaysia to Australia to marry an Anglo-Australian man she had met online, struggled for years to find friends. When they moved from Queensland to Melbourne, Winnie joined the group for Malaysian mothers, hoping to find "some quality friends that we can exchange heart." She particularly hoped to find someone married to an Anglo-Australian "because we're both in-between and because we both understand both cultures." In our interview, Winnie expressed her deep sense of relief from the realisation that other Asian migrants also found it difficult to make friends in Australia:

> Feel great, I feel [inhales] oh my goodness! After all these years, I finally feel that I find some friends. I'm not alone, and I'm not the one who has mental issues because I see everyone [...] has a common issue, in the sense of making friends in Australia.

Winnie reported that her husband had told her she just needed to "try harder" to make friends, failing to understand the cultural and linguistic barriers, and racism, that Winnie encountered. Winnie's participation in the group helped her husband place their experience in a broader context, which had eased an area of conflict in their marriage.

> He does understand now that... [...] It's from your background, same background, that's where you can find the best friends, and just instantly you trust each other, you are just comfortable [...] because you know each other's culture.

Before posting on the group, Katrin had seen her homesickness as a personal failure: "sometimes you think: am I failing, should I just move back home?" She asked the German mothers in the group, "Is this normal? Will it ever go away?" The responses she received in the group discussion and through private messages reassured her that it was a common experience and not a personal failure:

> Everyone just wrote, 'I don't think it will ever stop.' So, and that kind of makes you feel better [...] People were like, 'the grass is not greener on the other side, and it just won't go away. You just got to learn to live with it, unfortunately, so don't think your life's too bad.' So that was actually quite helpful. It sounds not helpful, but it actually was.

Women did not necessarily have to initiate discussions to benefit from them. Siobhan said she was "too private" to post about herself, and Lisa described herself as too "internal" to want "everything out there" but they were still able to derive a sense of relief or solidarity from witnessing others' posts. Siobhan explained:

> So even though I'm not commenting, or I'm not putting my own stuff out there, seeing that other people are doing it, seeing that other people have those feelings [...] I do like to see – not that I like to see that people are lonely but I like to see that people, you know, you're not the only person feeling that way. So that's the value of the groups really, isn't it? To see that, and thank god some people are brave enough to post on it.

Women understood the importance of responding, even just clicking 'like' on a comment, "just to show I understand, I hear you" (Siobhan). The 'like' button and discussion space are "emotional affordances" (Bareither 2019) of the groups, which enable members to enact empathy and solidarity. In so doing, they co-construct an imagined community of migrant mothers to which they belong, members of which share similar emotional responses to migrant motherhood.

For non-Anglophone mothers, a key area of "failure" was their unfulfilled desire to pass on their heritage language to their children. For some, this appeared to be a minor frustration, but others felt, like the Australian-based Spanish-speaking mothers in Mejía's 2015 study, that their language "is the most valuable thing they can pass on to their children" (p. 32) and thus judged themselves harshly if they had not (yet) raised bilingual children. Heritage languages in Australia have often been seen more as a hindrance to migrant assimilation than as an important skill (Eisenchlas et al. 2013), and there is thus little institutional support for migrants who want their children to learn them. Women recounted facing incomprehension, indifference, and judgement from their Anglophone partner and their partner's family, and resistance from their children. Some women's parents became "angry" (Annika) or "upset" (Katrin) at their grandchildren's refusal to speak their language. The need to navigate this maelstrom of emotions, in the context of non-existent institutional support for language learning, was a key driver for non-Anglophone women to join the migrant maternal groups.

Women's role as "transmitters of ethnic culture in their child-rearing" (Anthias 2012, p. 106), particularly, but not exclusively, in a migrant context, is well-documented (see also Manohar 2013a; Gedalof 2009; Anthias & Yuval-Davis 1989). Raising a bilingual child who could communicate with non-Anglophone family and access employment or education overseas was seen by some women as a marker of good migrant motherhood. The mothers' ambitions of raising bilingual children related to their aspiration to build a trans-national identity (Utomo 2014, p. 176), which would link them to their children through a shared language. For example, while Sabina noted that fluency in Swedish might enable her son to access free tertiary education in Sweden, her main motivation for teaching her son Swedish was in fact emotional, or identity-based. Sabina recalled her husband's assessment of Swedish as "such an insignificant language compared to Spanish,"[2] to which Sabina declared, "you can't really say that about a language." Explaining the centrality of language to her identity, she said, "when I'm old and senile and have forgotten everything else, I'll speak Swedish." Teaching her son Swedish was a means of establishing a link between him and this core part of herself. Petra explained how her son's exclusion from the German playgroup felt like a personal failure, which her Anglo-Australian husband struggled to comprehend:

My husband struggles to [understand] why it was so important to me. [...] I felt, I tried to do this bilingual thing, and I kind of felt I'd failed or something. It was a sore spot.

In contrast to her husband's response, the German mothers' group understood the importance of language transmission to Petra. Previously Petra had been ambivalent about co-ethnic friendships; this experience changed her mind: "I had to revise my view [...] it's actually not a bad thing to know some Germans. It can actually be helpful." The groups gave mothers access to advice on raising bilingual children, language-based playgroups, and opportunities to maintain their own linguistic proficiency, as well as emotional solidarity and support.

Disconnection

A combination of missing home and disrupted connections with friends, family, and culture left many women with a yearning for homely familiarity and security, which they found in the groups. Eva described the Swedish group as "a bit of home, but nearby." Lina described recently arrived Swedish migrants in the group as feeling "home-y to me, so it's like Sweden is not that far away." This feeling was enhanced by the fact that fellow group members were not just Swedish but also "Swedish people who have travelled, just like me." Gemma described the nostalgic feelings precipitated by seeing posts on the British group about "watching Wimbledon" on the television. The sense of comfort, closeness, and connection had a familial sense for Grainne, who explained: "When you meet up with them, I think they... they're just... they feel a bit more like family." Communication between members was described as "easy" and "comfortable" in comparison to more fraught interchanges with Australians. Annika recalled collecting an item from a German mother she had never met before, "you just click, you know, we talk, it was fun, it was like we talk about the same things and it felt easy, you know, sometimes maybe not so easy with Australian mums." Archana, too, felt their shared background facilitated a greater sense of connection with Indian mothers:

> Culturally we come from a similar background, so there are some issues which are probably very ... [...] Indian in nature, at the core. So, I think that's where it probably becomes more comfortable. [...] I feel it's just a little easier to connect, like I said I have a few Australian friends, very few ...

The groups can be "a bit of home," and they can also make people "feel more at home" (Michelle). In a migrant maternal context where isolation is widespread, and social networks have often been ruptured, the groups offer the possibility of support, information, and sociality, creating a reassuring sense of comfort, security, and belonging. Significantly, this comfort was felt even by participants who rarely interacted in the group. "Just knowing that they're there, it's a bit of a comfort," Siobhan explained. Grainne described the group as a "comfort cushion," while Sabina used the image of a "fire extinguisher – you might never use it but [...] you're happy it's there." Winnie explained, "Even though I don't use them every day, but when I need them, they are there." Priya noted that, as a migrant, it was "comforting to know that you've got people around you." She described feeling "more at peace, definitely, knowing that people are just literally around the corner." The participants' words resonate with the literature around homesickness (Scharp et al. 2016) and home-building (Hage 1997), which indicates that "comfort and safety are integral to defining what 'home' means to homesick individuals" (Scharp et al. 2016, p. 1191) and that "social support acts as a buffer against the negative effects of homesickness" (p. 1192).

Relational settlement: Finding belonging through social relationships

Both migration and motherhood rupture women's established social networks at the precise time their need for support, advice, information, empathy, and companionship increases. Building new social networks around their new maternal role is a critical means by which mothers re-shape their world following the momentous upheaval that is the transition to motherhood. New mothers reach for each other to create a community of mothers, either in their local area or in online communities or blogging networks (Arnold & Martin 2016; Bell & Ribbens 1994; Madge & O'Connor 2006; Strange et al. 2014a). Similarly, migrants work hard to make social connections, to build networks and communities in which they can find friendship, empathy, fun, and belonging. Much migration research focuses on the material benefits to be found via these connections, using a social capital framework (for example, Patulny 2015; Ryan 2011). While material and emotional benefits may be interconnected, this chapter has focused primarily on the affective connections between migrant mothers and the emotional affordances of the groups.

While women sought emotional support in the groups, as described above, the ruptures in their social networks wrought by migration and/or motherhood had also uncovered the pragmatic importance of social connections to building a workable life as a migrant mother. While women sought friends with whom they "got on" or "clicked" and had "something in common," they also looked for who lived nearby, could meet at convenient times, had children the same age, and other practical considerations. Celine hoped to find potential babysitters and people to help pick up her children from school, and she therefore focused her attention on local people. Celine had previous experience of migrating from the UK to New Zealand:

> I was part of a migrant mums group there, so I had lots of migrant mums around, and I used to go and knit with them, because that's what you do [both laugh]. So, I'll do whatever! I'll knit if that's what you do to go and meet people!

Women sought out social connections for their own benefit (seeking friendship, empathy, solidarity, belonging), for their children's benefit (friendships, language acquisition, identity), and for the benefit of their whole family (creating a social structure, creating a sense of belonging for the whole family). Relational settlement, therefore, involves forms of sociality that are multimodal and multilayered, operating at different levels of intimacy. Casual contacts, and social interactions that function as a kind of entertainment, carry affective resonances that belie their apparent superficiality. Intermediate ties – people who are neither family nor friends but who can be relied on for emotional and practical support – are particularly important for migrants building a life in a new place. Finally, women spoke about intimate friendships they had developed, or hoped to develop, around the group. Distinguishing between these levels of sociality facilitates a nuanced analysis of the types of social relations and structures that have been disrupted by migration and motherhood, and of the different ways migrant mothers utilise the affordances of the Facebook groups to rebuild their social infrastructure.

Casual intimacy and culturally inflected banter

One of the challenges migrants face is the sense of having been "cut adrift from the social moorings secured by affective ties of family and friends, as well as community and place" (Yeoh & Khoo 1998, p. 172). Participants missed their close friendships but also noted the absence of casual connections with whom they could gossip, exercise, or go to the cinema. New mothers missed the sociality of the workplace and needed companionship during the day when many of their friends were at work. The migrant maternal online groups provided them with opportunities to start rebuilding "the social and community fabric in which their lives were embedded" (Yeoh & Khoo 1998, p. 172).

The migrant maternal groups offered a first step to rebuilding a social network: easy to access online, a sense of belonging generated by meeting the group's membership criteria, some commonalities to spark discussion, and opportunities to meet offline. For Celine, joining the group was a means to broaden her "social circle" by attending social events:

> It's just nice to know that you've got an invitation somewhere. So it's not that they are British, it's the fact that I've got an invitation and I happen to have got the invitation because I'm British.

Kate, an administrator of the Brazilian group, described the group of fellow single mothers she had met through the group as "just to go out girls, they're not like the friends I tell everything." Nevertheless, she cited these "go out girls" as one of the main benefits of participating in the group. Both the close friendships Kate had developed through the group and the casual social relationships formed there constituted important elements of her migrant maternal social infrastructure.

The groups afforded the possibility for light-hearted, playful chat, in online discussions and offline meet-ups. Priya described her Indian mothers' group as "a good place to just vent and talk about random stuff as well." Although she spoke earnestly about her role in facilitating support through the group, she explained "it can be a good distraction as well; it's not just a support group." She recalled the enjoyment of participating in a "random sort of chat or banter with people from the same background," like discussing plans for Valentine's Day, which she notes is "massive in India, even though it's not our festival." Her fellow administrator, Nisha, emphasised the importance of casual chat for encouraging women to participate in the group, as it enabled them to ask for support on more serious topics when they needed it. Susie recounted the "banter" from the offline British mothers' meet-up, discussing each other's clothes, familiar clothes shops, and sourcing "real English chocolate" in Australia. Kate likened watching activities in the group to the Brazilian soap operas she grew up with, providing light entertainment. Not necessarily intended to lead to deeper friendships, although they sometimes were a pathway to intimacy, these opportunities for banter were a significant form of culturally inflected social connection. Shared backgrounds make such banter possible. In turn, banter provides a connection to home and culture that lends it more affective weight. As Francisco-Menchavez (2018) observes in her study of a Filipina migrants' community in New York, "teasing, banter and laughter are just as important as the struggles" for producing what Manalansan (2005) calls "diasporic intimacy." Even at this casual level, the groups are "far more than a constellation of contacts and exchanges in social capital or a swapping of resources" (Francisco-Menchavez 2018, p. 99).

Intermediate intimacy: Supportive strangers and latent ties

> I feel like they are a bunch of strangers, but at the same time, they're a bunch of strangers that are very supportive to each other.
>
> (Grainne)

The intermediate nature of the groups was a recurring theme. In Karen's words, "it's not too close, but it's not far away either; it's just at your fingertips." The phrase "at your fingertips" might imply proximity, but in this context, Karen is referring to the fact that the group is accessible via her phone, which is often literally at her fingertips. Nevertheless, because the connection is via her phone, she is also able to turn it off or put it away, so it is not "too close." She is in control of the degree of connection. Karen's words appear to resonate with Turkle's assertion that "technology makes it easy to communicate when we wish and to disengage at will" (2011, p. 13), an affordance dubbed "volume control" by Baron (2008). Despite this desire for control, participants' experiences contradict Turkle's claims that digital connections create only the "illusion of companionship" (2011) and a "decline in empathy" (2016). While the digital connections manifest in the group may not always be expressions of deep friendship, they are more than an empty performance or illusion. The groups provide a conduit for empathy and support between people who might never have met in person but who consider common membership in the group to be sufficient grounds for providing support. The relationships developed through the groups seemed to exist in an intermediate space between stranger-ship (Horgan 2012) and friendship, between weak and strong ties (Petróczi et al. 2007). The groups afforded opportunities to interact casually both online and offline – for example, answer each other's questions or chat at a playgroup – without it developing into a friendship.

Much of the significance of those intermediate relationships lies in the "latent ties" which underlie them. A latent tie, in this context, is a potential relationship of obligation, support, or empathy, derived from mutual membership of a group. It can be activated by a request for information or help, but prior to that, it has only a latent value. Haythornthwaite (2005) established the concept of latent ties as connections which are "technically possible but not yet activated socially" (p. 137); for example, the potential connections created by the infrastructure of a departmental email list. In a Facebook group, the shared visibility of online interactions affords an awareness of those latent ties and what they might offer. This awareness produced a specific sense of security through interdependence. Women witnessed each other offering and receiving support and knew that they could activate it if they needed it. Such support was available immediately and was not dependent on developing a relation-ship or time spent in the group. As Gemma explained, "straightaway you could just join the group and post something, and you'll get that back straightaway." Immediacy is particularly important to migrants who have not had the opportunity to build trusting relationships.

Petra described how she had been part of the German mothers' group for a while, without seeking emotional support. When a distressing incident occurred at the playgroup she organised through the group, she instantly received meaningful support:

> We're not close friends, but I think there's a certain connection that grows over the years. You don't have to be, like, deeply connected at all times, but when there's someone needs, there's a connection. You know, someone needs us now. Because I was pretty devastated, and they picked that up […] And I think that's because we're from the same culture, I think that's why it was, yeah.

South Asian mothers in Melbourne put together a roster to cook and deliver meals to a struggling mother who had contacted the group administrator for help. On another occasion, they helped a mother locked out of her apartment with her children. Brazilian mothers helped find employment for members' husbands who had lost the jobs on which the family's visa depended. All members, whether they had organised, received, offered, or witnessed acts of support or social connection, were aware of the potential for the group to respond to members' needs. The women make use of the affordances of the group to co-construct a sense of security through interdependence, a "safety net" (Gemma) of other migrant mothers, which builds a sense of home. Winnie explained:

Even though I don't use them every day, but when I need them, they are there. I know where to go if it's something that I just want to ask Chinese – maybe just my culture thing or whatever – they are there. And I can find people to instantly meet up, if I want to meet someone who speaks my language. So, I think that is really important, helpful, and makes me feel like I'm home. [...] I don't feel like I'm so lonely, I find that people will still understand me and are here to support me if I need to.

A shared identity as migrant mothers from a particular background intersects with the "mediated intimacy" (Chambers 2013) of online sociality to create a migrant maternal safety net consisting of latent, intermediate ties. In this sense, it is a digital extension of the migrant community building described by Manohar (2013b) as "a fundamentally gendered settlement activity" in which migrant mothers use "gendered labor" to "construct a dynamic community" (p. 25) as a response to the "loss of the extended kin safety network" (p. 30). Building these networks is a central means by which migrant mothers create the material and emotional stability they need to build a sense of home for themselves and their family (Gedalof 2009).

"Exchanging hearts": Pathways to friendship

Beyond their role as a "safety net" (Gemma) or "comfort cushion" (Grainne), the groups afforded the possibility of close friendships, which many women had struggled to form since migrating to Australia or becoming mothers. Usha recalled posting on the group for Indian mothers, looking for mothers in her locality who might want to meet. From the resulting meet-up, she developed a close friendship, and the two families celebrated Diwali together. Friendships that started in the group gained greater intimacy when they started to meet in person, when they shared approaches to parenting or leisure interests, had children of the same age and/or gender, or derived ongoing practical or emotional support from the friendship. For example, Diya described a friendship that started in the UK/Irish mothers' group, but then grew beyond it, based on common interests, children who are the same age, and shared "parenting ethos":

We met [...] on the group, yeah, and then we met up at one of the meet-ups. And then, we meet up individually outside of the meet-ups, and obviously our babies are now the same age so we can have playdates and things. [...] We've got more in common, [...] we're into similar things, or we have a similar parenting ethos or yeah... we're both really into healthy food and cooking, and so we'll share tips on that sort of stuff. So, we have got more in common, and I guess that's why we've become friends. As opposed to some of the other women, who I'll mainly just see at a meet-up and say 'hi.'

Lina, too, distinguished between "acquaintances" and "friends" based on her desire to meet friends, regularly, outside group interactions:

> I want to meet the ones that I formed a connection with in that Swedish group. I want to see them at least every month, at one point. We definitely always go to each other's birthday parties. So, they are friends.

For Stefanie, while she cited her mother as her primary source of personal emotional support, she had come to rely almost entirely on her circle of fellow German mothers for support around issues relating to her children. Petra was her closest friend from the group, which she attributed to the fact they both worked nearly full-time, unlike many other German mothers in her social circle, and happened to work near each other. This made it easy for them to meet, for example, for a coffee on their way to work and discuss the challenges of managing work, long commutes, and child-raising.

Becoming 'Facebook friends' was also cited as a step on the pathway towards 'real' friendship. As a performative act, becoming Facebook friends can be a ritualised public display of a personal connection, involving rapid and intense self-disclosure (Chambers 2013, p. 166; Lambert 2013). By contrast, members of the same group can interact for months or even years while retaining more control over personal disclosures. As research suggests people interpret self-disclosure online as representative of intimacy, leading to reciprocal disclosure (Jiang et al. 2013), this move to Facebook friendship can be characterised as an escalation of intimacy.

The groups offer a sense of hope and the possibility of friendship for women struggling to form close friendships since migrating to Australia. Participants discussed group-related interactions that might blossom into more intimate friendships. Winnie had joined the group hoping to find "quality friends" with whom she could "exchange hearts." While she didn't feel she had yet achieved that, she had found "quite a close friend" through the group and continued to hope for more. Kavita similarly imagined the future of a friendship from the group and how it might move up the scale of intimacy:

> We've done a few things; we've been to each other's kids' birthdays, our blokes have met, we'll probably do more things together. You know, you just kind of get to that stage where you know, as your network or your foundation, relationship develops, you get more overlap, and then it just becomes really natural, doesn't it, after a while?

These examples make visible the temporal and developmental nature of maternal friendships as they move from online interactions to in-person exchanges, drawing their children and spouses along with them. These friendships help build a broader social infrastructure by drawing their families closer together. Participants were conscious of the work involved in moving friendships along a scale of intimacy. While the group-based interactions, whether online or offline, were in some ways seen as contrived or mediated by the frame of the group, they provided a potential pathway to deeper, more "natural" friendships.

Conclusion

Many studies of migrant maternal isolation end with calls for more social support but rarely define the kind of support needed or how it might be delivered. By dissecting the different layers of sociality operating in the groups, and emphasising their creation by and for migrant mothers themselves, this chapter suggests that when migrant mothers build their own communities of support they gain sustenance from opportunities for casual sociality, relationships of interdependence, exchanges of empathy, and pathways to more intimate friendships.

Some feminist migration scholars have characterised migrant women's community-building as "a fundamentally gendered settlement activity" and "an integral component of their care work" as migrant wives and mothers (Manohar 2013b, drawing on Hondagneu-Sotelo 1994). Their implication is that this gendered labour is primarily for the benefit of partners and children. However, in line with the idea that mothers may sustain a "selfhood outside of and beyond motherhood" (O'Reilly 2016, p. 135), I suggest that migrant mothers' community-building is also designed to meet women's own needs for intimacy, friendship, and support (Francisco-Menchavez 2018; Williams Veazey 2019). Participating in the groups is simultaneously a practice of care for their family and for themselves, and an act of what Francisco-Menchavez (2018) has termed "horizontal caring" for other migrant women.

Migrant mothers, at the intersection of maternal isolation and migrant loneliness, use migrant maternal groups to rebuild their multiply disrupted social infrastructure and make a home for themselves in a new place. These moves towards relational settlement encompass multilayered sociality: casual, intermediate, and intimate. Each level of sociality contributes to a deeper and multilayered sense of belonging: to a local community, an online community, and a transnational 'imagined community' of mothers drawing on common experiences and imaginaries of nationality, migration, and motherhood. New belongings are co-constructed in relationships with other migrant mothers and in utilising the emotional affordances of the online groups. Emotions such as failure, homesickness, guilt, disconnection, and insecurity worked against participants' ability to feel 'at home' in Australia. Participating in migrant maternal communities helped participants not to overcome these emotions but to reconcile them with the possibility of belonging. These are the processes of relational and affective settlement.

Notes

1 Some of the content of this chapter has been previously published as Williams Veazey, L. (2019). Glocalised motherhood: Sociality and affect in migrant mothers' online communities. *Feminist Encounters: A Journal of Critical Studies in Culture and Politics, 3(1–2)*, 1–15. It is reproduced here under the *Creative Commons Attribution License.*
2 Born in Latin America, Sabina speaks fluent Spanish, Swedish, and English.

References

Ahmed, S., Castaneda, C., Fortier, A.-M., & Sheller, M. (2003). Introduction: Uprootings/regroundings: Questions of home and migration. In S. Ahmed, C. Castaneda, A.-M. Fortier, & M. Sheller (Eds.), *Uprootings/regroundings: Questions of home and migration* (1st ed, pp. 1–19). Oxford: Bloomsbury Publishing.
Alinejad, D., & Ponzanesi, S. (2020). Migrancy and digital mediations of emotion. *International Journal of Cultural Studies*, 23(5), 621–638. doi:10.1177/1367877920933649.
Anthias, F. (2012). Transnational mobilities, migration research and intersectionality. *Nordic Journal of Migration Research*, 2(2), 102–110. doi:10.2478/v10202-011-0032-y.
Anthias, F., & Yuval-Davis, N. (1989). Introduction. In N. Yuval-Davis, F. Anthias, & J. Campling (Eds.), *Woman-nation-state*. Palgrave Macmillan: London.
Arnold, L. B., & Martin, B. A. (Eds.). (2016). *Taking the village online: Mothers, motherhood, and social media*. Bradford, ON: Demeter Press.
Australian Institute of Family Studies. (2009). *Growing up in Australia, the longitudinal study of Australian children: Annual report 2008–09*. Retrieved from https://www.dss.gov.au/sites/default/files/documents/lsac_ar_08-09.pdf.
Balaji, A. B., Claussen, A. H., Smith, D. C., Visser, S. N., Morales, M. J., & Perou, R. (2007). Social support networks and maternal mental health and well-being. *Journal of Women's Health*, 16(10), 1386–1396. doi:10.1089/jwh.2007.CDC10.
Baldassar, L. (2015). Guilty feelings and the guilt trip: Emotions and motivation in migration and transnational caregiving. *Emotion, Space and Society*, 16, 81–89. doi:10.1016/j.emospa.2014.09.003.
Bandyopadhyay, M., Small, R., Watson, L. F., & Brown, S. (2010). Life with a new baby: How do immigrant and Australian-born women's experiences compare? *Australian and New Zealand Journal of Public Health*, 34(4), 412–421. doi:10.1111/j.1753-6405.2010.00575.x.
Baraitser, L. (2009). Mothers who make things public. *Feminist Review*, 93(93), 8–26. doi:10.1057/fr.2009.21.
Barclay, L., & Kent, D. (1998). Recent immigration and the misery of motherhood: A discussion of pertinent issues. *Midwifery*, 14(1), 4–9. doi:10.1016/S0266-6138(98)90108–90105.
Bareither, C. (2019). Doing emotion through digital media: An ethnographic perspective on media practices and emotional affordances. *Ethnologia Europaea*. doi:10.16995/ee.822.
Baron, N. S. (2008). *Always on: Language in an online and mobile world*. Oxford: Oxford University Press.
Bell, L., & Ribbens, J. (1994). Isolated housewives and complex maternal worlds – the significance of social contacts between women with young children in industrial societies. *The Sociological Review*, 42(2), 227–262.

Benza, S., & Liamputtong, P. (2014). Pregnancy, childbirth and motherhood: A meta-synthesis of the lived experiences of immigrant women. *Midwifery*, 30, 575–584. doi:10.1016/j.midw.2014.03.005.

Boccagni, P., & Baldassar, L. (2015). Emotions on the move: Mapping the emergent field of emotion and migration. *Emotion, Space and Society*, 16, 73–80. doi:10.1016/j.emospa.2015.06.009.

Chambers, D. (2013). *Social media and personal relationships: Online intimacies and networked friendship*. Basingstoke: Palgrave Macmillan.

Collins, P. H. (1991). The meaning of motherhood in Black culture and Black mother-daughter relationships. In P. Bell-Scott (Ed.), *Double stitch: Black women write about mothers & daughters*. Boston: Beacon Press.

De Silva, M. (2017). Making the emotional connection: Transnational eldercare circulation within Sri Lankan-Australian transnational families. *Gender, Place & Culture*, 1–16. doi:10.1080/0966369X.2017.1339018.

DeSouza, R. (2013). Regulating migrant maternity: Nursing and midwifery's emancipatory aims and assimilatory practices. *Nursing inquiry*, 20(4), 293–304. doi:10.1111/nin.12020.

Diminescu, D. (2008). The connected migrant: An epistemological manifesto. *Social Science Information*, 47(4), 565–579.

Döveling, K., Harju, A. A., & Sommer, D. (2018). From mediatized emotion to digital Affect cultures: New technologies and global flows of emotion. *Social Media + Society*, 4(1). doi:10.1177/2056305117743141.

Ebaugh, H., & Curry, M. (2000). Fictive kin as social capital in new immigrant communities. *Sociological Perspectives*, 43(2), 189–209. doi:10.2307/1389793.

Eisenchlas, S. A., Schalley, A. C., & Guillemin, D. (2013). The importance of literacy in the home language: The view from Australia. *SAGE Open*, 3(4). doi:10.1177/2158244013507270.

English, T., Davis, J., Wei, M., & Gross, J. J. (2017). Homesickness and adjustment across the first year of college: A longitudinal study. *Emotion*, 17(1), 1–5. doi:10.1037/emo0000235.

Francisco-Menchavez, V. (2018). *The labor of care: Filipina migrants and transnational families in the digital age*. University of Illinois Press.

Gedalof, I. (2009). Birth, belonging and migrant mothers: Narratives of reproduction in feminist migration studies. *Feminist Review*, 93(1), 81–100.

Gibson, L., & Hanson, V. L. (2013). 'Digital motherhood' *Chi '13 proceedings of the SIGCHI conference on human factors in computing systems* (pp. 313–322). New York: Association for Computing Machinery.

Gilmartin, M., & Migge, B. (2016). Migrant mothers and the geographies of belonging. *Gender, Place & Culture*, 23(2), 147–161. doi:10.1080/0966369X.2014.991700.

Gregory, T., Harman-Smith, Y., Sincovich, A., Wilson, A., & Brinkman, S. (2016). *It takes a village to raise a child: The influence and impact of playgroups across Australia*. Retrieved from https://playgroupaustralia.org.au/resource/it-takes-a-village-to-raise-a-child/.

Hage, G. (1997). At home in the entrails of the west. In H. Grace, G. Hage, L. Johnson, J. Langsworth, & M. Symonds (Eds.), *Home/world: Space, community and marginality in Sydney's west* (pp. 99–153). Annandale, NSW: Pluto Press.

Haythornthwaite, C. (2005). Social networks and internet connectivity effects. *Information, Communication & Society*, 8(2), 125–147. doi:10.1080/13691180500146185.

Hetherington, E., McDonald, S., Williamson, T., Patten, S. B., & Tough, S. C. (2018). Social support and maternal mental health at 4 months and 1 year postpartum: Analysis from the All Our Families cohort. *Journal of Epidemiology and Community Health*. doi:10.1136/jech-2017-210274.

Hondagneu-Sotelo, P. (1994). *Gendered transitions: Mexican experiences of immigration*. University of California Press.

hooks, b. (1984). *Feminist theory: From margin to center*. Cambridge, MA: South End Press.

Horgan, M. (2012). Strangers and strangership. *Journal of Intercultural Studies*, 33(6), 607–622. doi:10.1080/07256868.2012.735110.

Jiang, L. C., Bazarova, N. N., & Hancock, J. T. (2013). From perception to behavior: Disclosure reciprocity and the intensification of intimacy in computer-mediated communication. *Communication Research*, 40(1), 125–143. doi:10.1177/0093650211405313.

Johnson, S. (2017, 18/09/2017). Motherhood is tough enough without being isolated. *Huffpost AU*. Retrieved from https://www.huffingtonpost.com.au/samantha-johnson/we-need-to-reach-out-and-reassure-our-already-vulnerable-rural-mums_a_23212763/.

Kędra, J. (2020). Performing transnational family with the affordances of mobile apps: A case study of Polish mothers living in Finland. *Journal of Ethnic and Migration Studies*. doi:10.1080/1369183X.2020.1788383.

Lambert, A. (2013). *Intimacy and friendship on Facebook*. Basingstoke: Palgrave Macmillan.

Leahy-Warren, P., McCarthy, G., & Corcoran, P. (2012). First-time mothers: Social support, maternal parental self-efficacy and postnatal depression. *Journal of Clinical Nursing*, 21(3–4), 388–397. doi:10.1111/j.1365-2702.2011.03701.x.

Lee, K., Vasileiou, K., & Barnett, J. (2017). 'Lonely within the mother': An exploratory study of first-time mothers' experiences of loneliness. *Journal of Health Psychology*. doi:10.1177/1359105317723451.

Madge, C., & O'Connor, H. (2006). Parenting gone wired: Empowerment of new mothers on the internet? *Social & Cultural Geography*, 7(2), 199–220. doi:10.1080/14649360600600528.

Manohar, N. N. (2013a). Mothering for class and ethnicity: The case of Indian professional immigrants in the United States. *Advances in Gender Research*, 17, 159–185. doi:10.1108/S1529-2126(2013)0000017011.

Manohar, N. N. (2013b). Support networks, ethnic spaces, and fictive kin: Indian immigrant women constructing community in the United States. *AAPI Nexus: Policy, Practice and Community*, 11(1–2), 25–55. doi:10.17953/appc.11.1-2.t81xj18224638u44.

Manalansan, M. (2005). Migrancy, modernity, mobility: Quotidian struggles and queer diasporic intimacy. In E. Luibhéid, & L. Cantú (Eds.), *Queer migrations: Sexuality, U.S. citizenship, and border crossings* (pp. 146–160). Minneapolis: University of Minnesota Press.

McLaren, L. (2018). The excruciating loneliness of being a new mother. *Todays Parent*. Retrieved from https://www.todaysparent.com/baby/postpartum-care/the-excruciating-loneliness-of-being-a-new-mother/.

Mejía, G. (2015). Language usage and culture maintenance: A study of Spanish-speaking immigrant mothers in Australia. *Journal of Multilingual and Multicultural Development*, 37(1),22–39. doi:10.1080/01434632.2015.1029931.

Miller, T. (2005). *Making sense of motherhood: A narrative approach*. Cambridge University Press.

Moore, J., & Riley, L. (2010). Aboriginal mother yarns. In S. Goodwin, & K. Huppatz (Eds.), *The good mother* (pp. 175–193). Sydney: Sydney University Press.

O'Reilly, A. (2016). *Matricentric feminism: Theory, activism, practice.* Bradford, ON: Demeter Press.

Patulny, R. (2015). A spectrum of integration: Examining combinations of bonding and bridging social capital and network heterogeneity among Australian refugee and skilled migrants. In L. Ryan, U. Erel, & A. D'Angelo (Eds.), *Migrant capital: Networks, identities and strategies* (pp. 207–229). London: Palgrave Macmillan.

Petróczi, A., Nepusz, T., & Bazsó, F. (2007). Measuring tie-strength in virtual social networks. *Connections*, 27(2), 39–52.

Raman, S., Srinivasan, K., Kurpad, A., Dwarkanath, P., Ritchie, J., & Worth, H. (2014). 'My mother…my sisters…and my friends': Sources of maternal support in the perinatal period in urban India. *Midwifery*, 30(1), 130–137. doi:10.1016/j.midw.2013.03.003.

Rich, A. (1976). *Of woman born: Motherhood as experience and institution.* New York: Norton.

Rogan, F., Shmied, V., Barclay, L., Everitt, L., & Wyllie, A. (1997). 'Becoming a mother' – developing a new theory of early motherhood. *Journal of advanced nursing*, 25(5), 877–885. doi:10.1046/j.1365-2648.1997.1997025877.x.

Ryan, L. (2011). Migrants' social networks and weak ties: Accessing resources and constructing relationships post-migration. *The Sociological Review*, 59(4), 707–724. doi:10.1111/j.1467-954X.2011.02030.x.

Scharp, K. M., Paxman, C. G., & Thomas, L. J. (2016). "I want to go home": Homesickness experiences and social-support-seeking practices. *Environment and Behavior*, 48(9), 1175–1197. doi:10.1177/0013916515590475.

Schmied, V., Black, E., Naidoo, N., Dahlen, H. G., & Liamputtong, P. (2017). Migrant women's experiences, meanings and ways of dealing with postnatal depression: A meta-ethnographic study. *PLOS ONE*, 12(3), e0172385. doi:10.1371/journal.pone.0172385.

Scott, D., Brady, S., & Glynn, P. (2001). New mother groups as a social network intervention: Consumer and maternal and child health nurse perspectives. *The Australian Journal of Advanced Nursing*, 18(4), 23–29.

Seefat-van Teeffelen, A., Nieuwenhuijze, M., & Korstjens, I. (2011). Women want proactive psychosocial support from midwives during transition to motherhood: A qualitative study. *Midwifery*, 27(1), e122–e127. doi:10.1016/j.midw.2009.09.006.

Strange, C., Fisher, C., Howat, P., & Wood, L. (2014a). The essence of being connected: The lived experience of mothers with young children in newer residential areas. *Community, Work & Family*, 17(4), 486–502. doi:10.1080/13668803.2014.935704.

Stroebe, M., Schut, H., & Nauta, M. (2015). Homesickness: A systematic review of the scientific literature. *Review of General Psychology*, 19(2), 157–171. doi:10.1037/gpr0000037.

Stroebe, M., Schut, H., & Nauta, M. H. (2016). Is homesickness a mini-grief? Development of a dual process model. *Clinical Psychological Science*, 4(2), 344–358. doi:10.1177/2167702615585302.

Thurber, C. A., & Walton, E. A. (2012). Homesickness and adjustment in university students. *Journal of American College Health*, 60(5), 415–419. doi:10.1080/07448481.2012.673520.

Turkle, S. (2011). *Alone together: Why we expect more from technology and less from each other.* New York: Basic Books.

Turkle, S. (2016). *The empathy gap: Digital culture needs what talk therapy offers.* Washington: Psychotherapy Networker, Inc.

Utomo, A. (2014). Mother tongue, mothering, and (transnational) identity: Indonesian mothers in Canberra, Australia. *ASEAS – Austrian Journal of South-East Asian Studies*, 7(2), 165–182. doi:10.14764/10.ASEAS-2014.2-3.

Vermot, C. (2015). Guilt: A gendered bond within the transnational family. *Emotion, Space and Society*, 16, 138–146. doi:10.1016/j.emospa.2015.04.001.

Ward, C. (2004). Migrant mothers and the role of social support when child rearing. *Contemporary Nurse*, 16(1–2),74–85. doi:10.5172/conu.16.1-2.74.

Westcott, H. (2014). Imaginary friends: Migrants' emotional accounts about friends outside Australia. *Australian Journal of Social Issues*, 47(1), 87–103.

Westcott, H., & Vazquez Maggio, M. L. (2016). Friendship, humour and non-native language: Emotions and experiences of professional migrants to Australia. *Journal of Ethnic and Migration Studies*, 42(3), 503–518. doi:10.1080/1369183X.2015.1064764.

Wilding, R. (2006). 'Virtual' intimacies? Families communicating across transnational contexts. *Global Networks*, 6(2), 125–142. doi:10.1111/j.1471-0374.2006.00137.x.

Wilding, R., Baldassar, L., Gamage, S., Worrell, S., & Mohamud, S. (2020). Digital media and the affective economies of transnational families. *International Journal of Cultural Studies*, 23(5), 639–655. doi:10.1177/1367877920920278.

Wilkins, C. (2006). A qualitative study exploring the support needs of first-time mothers on their journey towards intuitive parenting. *Midwifery*, 22(2), 169–180. doi:10.1016/j.midw.2005.07.001.

Williams Veazey, L. (2019). Glocalised motherhood: Sociality and affect in migrant mothers' online communities. *Feminist Encounters: A Journal of Critical Studies in Culture and Politics*, 3(1–2), 09. doi:10.20897/femenc/5915.

Williams Veazey, L. (forthcoming). Mothers in the middle: Rethinking 'middling' migration as relational. In S. Robertson, & R. Roberts (Eds.), *Migrants 'in-between': Rethinking privilege and social mobility in middle-class migration*. Routledge.

Yeoh, B. S. A., & Khoo, L.-M. (1998). Home, work and community: Skilled international migration and expatriate women in Singapore. *International Migration*, 36(2), 159–186. doi:10.1111/1468-2435.00041.

4 Digital community mothering

Gendered digital labour and meta-maternal practices

Introduction

Nisha

By the time we speak in 2016, Nisha is a seasoned migrant, having left India in 2004 to follow her husband's work in the IT industry, first to Canada, then the United States, where they lived in four different cities in three years and welcomed their first child into the world. In 2008, they moved to Melbourne, where, after a period of disappointment and adjustment of expectations, they settled and had a second child. Central to her initial disappointment was the relatively poor internet connection they experienced in Australia in 2008. Nisha recalled, "I was just so used to, like, even if I don't have people around me, at least I have the internet; I could stay connected with people and friends. So it was really, really alienating when we first moved here." When we talk via video call, Nisha exudes a warm effervescence. She is quick to laugh and has clearly developed strategies to gather the social connections she needs. In the United States, she'd head straight for the local library and offer to volunteer, knowing she wouldn't be around long enough to find paid work, and had become part of a network of Indian mother bloggers.

I ask her what difference it would make to her life if the South Asian mothers' group she runs no longer existed. She gasps, then laughs. "I would be so lost without it! [...] Every time I attend an event or I organise something, I come away with at least one or two new friends. This group is such an important part of my life; I can't imagine it not being there because for me it's like my third baby." She laughs again. "Which is why I try so hard to keep it nice and happy. It's almost like the way I want my girls to be happy." And she does work hard at it. Until she started working two jobs last year, Nisha says, she was "online pretty much all the time [...] always monitoring the group." As well as friendship, her role as the creator and administrator of the group has brought Nisha visibility and recognition in the community. When I run through my spiel about the limits of anonymity in a study like this, she interrupts me, laughing, "Don't worry about it! I went to a party yesterday and I ran into someone and she recognised me from my face, and she goes 'I know you,' and I'm like, 'you do?' and she's like, 'yeah, I see your posts and everything, I'm on your group' and [...] that happens so many times."

This chapter focuses on the role of the administrators in creating and curating the groups as sites of social connection, information exchange, and identity exploration. Studies of online communities have tended to focus on the experiences of end users, overlooking "the very real labour of building and sustaining virtual communities" (D. Bell 2007, p. 255). Chapter 3 explored the emotional affordances (Bareither 2019) of the migrant maternal online groups. This chapter outlines how these emotional affordances are shaped by the groups' administrators. Businesses and non-profit agencies appoint professional community managers "to build and maintain brand loyalty by cultivating a dedicated community through social media, live social events, and strategic communication with consumers" (De Winter et al. 2017, p. 37). In the participative internet era (Fuchs 2014, p. 44), individual Facebook users, having made use of the user-friendly functionality to create a group, may find themselves in a similar, if unpaid and differently motivated, role. The level of intervention undertaken by administrators of more active groups was often unforeseen at the point of the group's creation. As groups surpassed their original aim of meeting the needs of a small group of peers, the administrators took on more intentional stewardship roles, becoming 'accidental community managers.' I use this term to distinguish it from the role of professional community manager, but, as this chapter will demonstrate, there is much that is intentional in their practices.

Community management is often undervalued and not recognised as skilled work. The 2019 Australian Community Managers survey found that 82 per cent of respondents hold a post-school qualification (compared to 56 per cent of the Australian population) and yet many report salaries under the national average as well as feelings of their role being "marginalised" (p. 43). Online community management is a "feminised profession" due to the centrality of "communication, care, and emotional labor" to the role (De Winter et al. 2017, p. 40). Successful community management relies on empathetic and nurturing behaviours, which are often naturalised as feminine qualities and therefore undervalued and underpaid (De Winter et al. 2017, p. 42; Duffy & Schwartz 2018). A 2019 survey of professional online community managers in Australia found that 71 per cent are women, a similar gender balance to that found in nursing and carework (Australian Community Managers 2019). At the same time, Jacobson (2017) argues, the analytic and technical skills which are equally necessary for successful community management are de-emphasised because – as masculine or neutrally coded skills – they do not fit the narrative that community management is naturally more suited to women (p. 112). In the migrant maternal groups, many of the administrators reported their spouse's lack of interest, disparagement or even resentment of their online community work. Maria, administrator of the Spanish-speaking mothers' group, said her husband resented the time she spent on the group as time away from their family, telling her, "we don't have that amount of time together to be wasting time in something that doesn't benefit us."

In Chapter 2, we saw how Ana characterised herself as the "proud mum" of the Brazilian mothers' group. In a similar vein, Nisha described the South Asian mothers' group as her "third baby." These maternal analogies are telling, both in terms of how the participants conceptualise their role and practices as administrators of the group, and for what this tells us about online community management more broadly. Even when community managers are not mothers, as they are in this study, the role is often perceived as having a maternal quality. In her study of professional community managers, Jacobson (2017) notes the prevalence of parenting metaphors in their descriptions of their work. Ng's *Online community management for dummies* also places community managers in the role of metaphorical parents: "There's an expression that unruly children crave discipline. This is kind of the case with online communities. Online community members are not unruly children by a long shot, but they do need to be molded and guided" (2012, p. 80).

Venessa Paech, founder of the Australian Community Managers network, has noted that professional online community managers are sometimes referred to as "our mother hen" or "our den mother" by other employees (Bogle 2018). On the one hand, this maternal terminology has the effect of devaluing the skillset required for such work, as motherhood itself is devalued as coming naturally to women, involving menial yet emotionally fulfilling tasks (Smart 1996), rather than a skilled role involving the development of conceptual, practical and psychological skills (Ruddick 1980). On the other hand, the maternal terminology also contains a suggestion of power and leadership. Motherhood, Ruddick suggests, is "a poignant conjunction of power and powerlessness," and the same could be said of online community management. Online community managers, whether paid or unpaid, hold significant power within the communities they manage. As Paech (2012) notes:

> Working as a community manager, I have experienced this power. I have the ability to sever individuals from their virtual bodies and disengage them from their self-selected community. In a technically simple move, we terminate an account and ban its owner from re-entry.
>
> (p. 29)

While maternal terminology may attempt to neutralise or soften the power of the community manager, it cannot entirely disguise it. A "mother hen" is, after all, a leader as much as she is a nurturer. The terminology may have patronising undertones, but, nevertheless, online community management has been a route by which women have risen to positions of influence within otherwise male-dominated tech companies.

This chapter explores the interplay of power and vulnerability, recognition and marginalisation, service and leadership in the experiences of the women who create and run these peer-led communities of migrant mothers in Australia. The first two sections explore the *boundary work* and *curation practices* they undertake to create spaces of trust, similarity, and sociality. Together, the administrators' boundary work and curation construct a "narrative of sameness" (Seligman 2012, p. 190) and a community norm of compassion among mothers, providing a shortcut to "in-group trust" (Weigert 2012, p. 178) that increases the groups' efficacy as vehicles for information-exchange, sociality, and belonging. The final section brings together concepts from feminist digital media scholarship, feminist migration scholarship, and Black feminist motherhood scholarship to consider the administrators' role and labour as community management, maternal leadership, digital house-wifery (Jarrett 2016), and digital community mothering. In analysing the 'meta-maternal' practices used by the administrators to construct and maintain these migrant maternal communities, this chapter makes visible the unpaid, gendered labour involved in this form of community-building and the gendered assumptions that naturalise this community-building as the task of migrant mothers.

Boundary work: Belonging, relevance, and trust

A community's boundaries are a public statement of what it signifies, its limits, and how it differentiates itself from other communities. The boundary is "the mask presented by the community to the outside world; it is the community's public face" (Cohen 1985, p. 71). Membership boundaries work to create a sense of belonging, by making clear "there are people who belong and people who do not" (McMillan & Chavis 1986, p. 9). A community's boundary is meaningful to those who are admitted, and to those who are denied entry. Administrators have the power to define the boundaries and to "grant or withdraw access to the community space" (Paech 2012, p. 29).

Administrators' first act of boundary setting, and the first boundary encountered by prospective members, is the nomenclature and description of the group. Group names communicate who is included in the group:

[Mothers/parents] from [country/region/linguistic group] living in [country, city, area].

The group's name is the "community's public face" (Cohen 1985) and indicates to potential members their likely inclusion or exclusion. For the smaller groups, the name and approval process were all the boundary work required to restrict membership to the intended people, as few people requested admittance who did not meet the membership criteria. As Nicole noted, "if a guy would look online, if it says, 'German mums,' he probably wouldn't want to join, because he thinks it's German mums." Larger, or more active, groups involved more active boundary maintenance.

When deciding whether to accept a potential member, administrators looked at the following evidence: the person's name (e.g., for clues to their gender and/or ethnicity) and Facebook profile (e.g., for visible information to suggest motherhood, place of residence, place of origin, or for clues they might be a fake profile or 'spammer'). Some undertook further searches on

Google or LinkedIn. If questions remained, administrators sent a private message to elicit more information or waited for the applicant to send a message with the necessary information. Some preferred to approve applicants who had been invited to join by existing members.[1] Most administrators also tried to attract new members by asking members to invite their friends, by posting in other online groups aimed at mothers or migrants, or by approaching people individually. One Indian mothers' group ran a prize draw to encourage members to invite their connections to join. Sabina posted about her Scandinavian group in her local generic online mothers' groups and approached mothers online who had "a Swedish-sounding name." In this way, the administrators sought to construct a community of the 'right' people: people who shared key roles, attachments, and experiences.

In our interviews, women discussed multiple attachments of belonging and intersecting identities, not all of which can be encapsulated in a single Facebook group. Careful curation by the administrators draws together people who share key, emotionally resonant, attachments. The following sections focus on two key axes of boundary maintenance and belonging: gender and geography.

Gendered boundaries: Constructing mothers as good digital citizens

Alongside national, ethnic, or linguistic criteria, gender was a primary marker by which administrators evaluated potential members' right to access the group. As discussed in Chapter 2, the groups varied in how strictly or intentionally they enforced their maternal exclusivity. The salience of gender extended beyond its intersection with parenthood, with members and administrators also drawing on notions of gendered sociality, support-seeking, and social media usage to justify the exclusion of men from these spaces. Personal experience, combined with ideological and policy frameworks, created a context in which mothers-only groups appeared either commonsensical or actively beneficial. Those in favour of mixed groups drew on equal parenting ideologies, which seemed to run counter to the lived experiences of most participants.

Administrators of groups with gender-based restrictions argued that fathers lacked the interest or need to join a group based around parenting, would not contribute the same understanding of parenting issues, and would be unavailable to meet due to being at work. Mothers, on the other hand, with their shared experiences of new motherhood, both needed support and were well-placed to offer it. Yasmin, the administrator of the Persian mothers' group, encapsulated some of these arguments:

> No matter how we look at it, in whatever culture, it's mainly the mum that looks after the child ... even if the father is hands-on, the mother is the one mainly involved. And the father cannot understand the mother like other mothers can. So I think it's important to have that sisterly connection.

For most participants, there was little sense of parenting as a "joint project" (Fox 2009, p. 141). The maternal focus of their group reflected their lived experience of parenting, with playgrounds and playgroups largely inhabited by women. Those gendered experiences of early parenthood are reflected in and reinforced by Australian norms, policies, and legislation. As outlined in Chapter 2, parenting and parents' support groups have long been considered gendered activities in Australia, and even today, groups run by councils for first-time parents are colloquially called "mothers' groups." While the primary carer of a newborn or adopted child in Australia is entitled to 18 weeks' leave paid at the national minimum wage, the "dad or partner" is entitled to two weeks' paid leave. Australian parental leave legislation refers to "primary carers (mainly birth mothers)" and lists among the aims of the legislation to "encourage women to continue to participate in the workforce," to "increase the time that fathers and partners take off work around the time of birth or adoption," and to "allow fathers and partners to take a greater share of caring responsibilities" ("Paid parental leave Act" 2010). These legislative aims reflect a status quo in which new fathers' time is more commonly spent at work than caring for their new child, while the opposite is true for new mothers. This helps to explain why, when women in this study formed groups from their personal contacts of people grappling with intensive needs of a newborn, those other people were mothers.

Only two administrators, one Swedish and one German, spoke strongly in support of involving fathers. For Jenni, this view reflected her attachment to gender equality, especially in relation to parenting. This mode of gender equality has been constructed as part of the Swedish national identity (Kvist & Peterson 2010) and embedded in Swedish social policy since the 1960s (Suwada 2017, pp. 97–105). Jenni maintains her commitment to shared parenting through her management of the Swedish parents' group:

> I don't want to bring my babies up in a world where it's like that. I want, I try to be very conscious about trying to be equal, trying to be … dads are just as much parents as mums.

For Tanja, the idea of restricting her German families' group to mothers appeared ridiculous and old-fashioned:

> What are you doing then if the dad is home? He's not allowed to join the group? Hey, in which times do we live?! No! [laughs] No!

This ideal of equal parenting ran counter to the experiences of most participants. Responses from participants in mixed groups indicated that fathers joined in much smaller numbers and interactions tended to be initiated by mothers. For Jenni and Tanja, the importance of their boundary work is in constructing spaces in which equal parenting is *possible*, even if it does not reflect their own experiences or the current local norms. Their curated spaces allow for minority modes of parenting in the present and for an imagined future in which equal parenting is commonplace.

Participating in the groups was also seen as a social strategy carried out by mothers on behalf of their other family members, as well as for their own benefit. Many women asserted their husbands' lack of interest in social media. For example, Archana explained:

> I tried inviting my husband to one or two groups, and he's like 'oh, just keep me out.' He's not even part of any WhatsApp groups of our families, so he's someone who doesn't want to be in all that. But I don't mind because I regularly go and tell him things.

When asked what their spouse thought of their migrant mothers' group, the most common response was that their husband either was not aware of the group or felt it had little relevance to him. For example, Usha stated,

> He doesn't even know that such a group exists. [...] He's not on Facebook, so he doesn't know about Facebook. And I would never... like, you know, discuss kind of things like this with him because ... you know, somewhere it is just so... irrelevant to his life.

Or, as Sheila succinctly stated: "Doesn't know. Doesn't care." Other participants reported more positive responses, with their husband acknowledging the benefit it brought to their family or to their wife. Stefanie mused, "I think he's happy for me," while Gemma reported her husband's appreciation of the group as an information resource for their family:

> I'll just post to this group and get the answer and he's like ... 'wow, this is good having a group where you can just get that kind of response so quickly.'

Some men were dismissive of the groups but still saw value in the information they could obtain from them. Maria, Sheila, and Pooja commented that despite describing the groups disparagingly as a "waste of time" (Maria), just a "bunch of women" (Pooja), or "internet friends" (Sheila), their husbands would ask their wives to find information in the groups:

> It's funny because when he needs something, he's like 'what if you ask in there, to see what happens?' But at the same time, he's like, 'you waste so much time and for you there is no [benefit].'
>
> (Maria)

Administrators like Maria commonly reported ambivalent responses from their spouse, particularly in relation to the amount of time they spent managing the groups, which was characterised by their spouse as excessive, despite professing support in principle. Ana said, "Oh he thinks it's fantastic. The only thing he says is: you work too much!" Nisha reported that her husband had initially dismissed the group as "wasting more time on Facebook" but more recently had expressed appreciation for her work:

> So he is quite supportive of it now, and when he comes across new people that are new to the area or new to Melbourne he tells his colleagues or whoever to look up the group, and he's like 'oh my wife is the admin and she's quite helpful.'

Nisha's husband thus recognises the importance of his wife's digital labour to their broader migrant community, which is explored later in the chapter.

For many participants, their husbands' negative or neutral responses to the group were linked not only to their gendered experiences of migration and parenting but more generally to their use of social media. Only four participants stated that their spouse was a frequent Facebook user. Like Archana's husband above, many left that whole domain to their wife. The active refusal by some of the spouses to participate in what may be viewed as a feminised use of online technology echoes Lohan's (2000) finding that men may differentiate their use of technology from women's usage as a means of reinforcing gendered dichotomies and hierarchies (p. 906). Archana's husband's refusal to participate in online social networks reinforced her role as the social facilitator for the family, echoing Yasmin's assertion that the mother "forms the social connections for the house." Maintaining transnational relationships after migration as well as nurturing new local social connections to facilitate relational settlement are both seen as women's responsibilities.

Women's responsibility for relational settlement activities was reinforced by notions of women-centred sociality. Participants noted their tendency to socialise with other women and their comfort with female-oriented groups. Lina noted, "it's just easier to talk to women," and Jyoti commented, "I think women tend to bond more with each other than we do with men." Priya suggested women "tend to reach out more, and talk more about stuff," Diya noted that women are "open to posting things that are personal or emotional," and Gemma maintained that women "share a lot more than guys do." Trust online has been connected to self-disclosure and empathy (Feng et al. 2004; Henderson & Gilding 2004), so women's characterisation of men as unlikely to empathise or make "personal or emotional" disclosures may compound their view of men as less trustworthy in these online spaces.

Participants drew on stereotypes that positioned women as social, co-operative, talkative, emotional, and willing to expose their vulnerability to obtain help. By contrast, their discussions positioned men as lacking the "urge" (Petra), willingness, or desire to engage in this kind of "social information foraging" (Pirolli 2009) or to make social connections for their family. These findings support Portwood-Stacer's contention that "the labor of online social networking" is an extension of women's "caring and relational labor involved in holding communities together":

Facebook mirrors the offline social world, in which women plan the get-togethers, send the birthday and holiday greetings, transmit the family gossip, and just generally stay present in everyone else's lives.

(2014, n.p.)

Ouellette and Wilson suggest this represents a digital "'second shift' of affective and domestic labour" (2011, p. 559). Archana's husband's refusal to join their families' WhatsApp groups supports Portwood-Stacer's observation that while men may abstain from this labour without sanction, they continue to benefit from their partner's labour. Women's capacity to withdraw from social media, to refuse to participate in this form of caring and relational labour, may be limited by the need to maintain "the standards of affective support they and their families expect" (Portwood-Stacer 2014, n.p.). In the context of migration, the women in this study described their use of social media to engage in caring and relational labour at a distance, for example, nurturing relationships between grandparents and their grandchildren; to effect their family's emplacement and affective settlement in their new home; and to build a community for themselves and their family. This is the gendered emotional and relational labour of migration.

Some participants argued women-only groups were more conducive to discussion of certain topics and to honest and sympathetic discussions. Women could better discuss relationships, sex, postnatal depression, breastfeeding, issues with in-laws, depression, domestic abuse, pregnancy, or feminism, they suggested, without men's presence. Manohar (2013) describes this exchange of gendered information in women-centred networks as creating "gendered social capital" (p. 36). While this sentiment was more commonly mentioned by administrators and members of the Indian and South Asian mothers' groups, British, Irish, German, Brazilian and Singaporean women also expressed similar views. Participants imagined a male gaze as judgemental, engendering a sense of discomfort or surveillance, not support. Gemma, a British migrant, suggested women would self-censor in the presence of men, for fear of being judged "neurotic females." The exclusion of men therefore helped to construct the groups as spaces of trust and safety for mothers. "I really want to keep this a safe space for mums," Nisha explained. She noted that while no fathers had yet requested to join her group, they had had requests from "single guys." Her fellow administrator, Priya, described these men as "random creeps." Their experiences of predatory male behaviour online, coupled with assumptions about gendered parenting roles, left women suspicious of men's motivations for accessing female-identified online groups: "What's this man doing here? Is he actually a dad [...] or does he have some other motive?" (Diya). While single women asking to join might be viewed as a fellow "nurturer" or "aunty" (Aditi), or potential childcare provider, single men were assumed to have nefarious intentions.

The specific context of online groups, and Facebook groups in particular, is significant here. Interactions in Facebook groups often occur in a context in which members share very little profile information, in contrast to interactions between 'Facebook friends,' in which there is an expectation of significant disclosure through photographs and status updates. Members of a group may only be able to see each other's name, profile photo, and limited information such as hometown or other groups they are in. In the absence of any other cues, such as body language or face to face communication, some women assumed that a man in a mothers' group is "some weirdo trying to connect with you online that you have no idea who they are" (Susie). In a playground or park, Susie explained, a man might still seem out of place attempting to join a group of mothers, but being able to "see them in the flesh" would encourage her to be more "accepting." This resonates with research into trust, where face-to-face communication has been found to engender greater, swifter, and more resilient levels of trust than audio, video, or text-based communication (Bos et al. 2002).

In conclusion, in the creation, maintenance, and justification of their gender-based boundaries, the groups simultaneously reflect and reproduce a gendered experience of parenting, sociality, trust, and support-seeking. At the intersection of parenting, community, and digital cultures, women construct themselves as good mothers, good community members, and good digital citizens. In the process of positioning themselves in this way, men are constructed as peripheral to the realms of parenting, emotion, and familial sociality. In setting and maintaining gender-based boundaries for their groups, the administrators are attempting to create spaces in which members can experience high levels of trust, relevance of content, and empathy based on common experience. At the same time, they have created spaces in which only women can perform this affective and relational labour of migration. Only Tanja and Jenni suggested that admitting men to these spaces might create the possibility of a different future, with responsibilities divided more equally between mothers and fathers.

Geographic boundaries: Residence and nationality

Chapter 2 outlined the three identifiers present in all the group names: role, residence, and origin. The administrators' boundary work to maintain the correct 'role' (mother, parent, family) is discussed above. The other two identifiers, origin and residence, required boundary work on two geographical axes: national (and less commonly ethnic/linguistic) identity and local residence. Perhaps surprisingly, given that tensions around national and ethnic belonging have been at the heart of some of the most bitter conflicts on the world stage, in these groups, discussions around national and ethnic identity were relatively relaxed and straightforward. By contrast, discussions around the importance, or otherwise, of members being located in the appropriate city or country revealed a tension at the heart of the groups: should the groups primarily act to create a localised sense of diasporic maternal belonging, or should they also provide a transnational resource for potential migrants? Should the focus be on facilitating settlement or facilitating mobility? While much has been made of the potential for "ambiguously located" social media to transcend geographic boundaries (Baym 2015, p. 81), or act as diasporic community spaces (Bernal 2014, p. 173), in these groups, local geography remained strongly salient and determinative.

In terms of national/ethnic identity, the nomenclature of the groups effectively maintained the boundary, such that administrators received few genuine (non-spam) requests from people who did not meet the criteria. In non-Anglophone groups, language created an additional boundary to entry or participation. Administrators used potential members' names and Facebook profiles to judge whether they appeared to be from the appropriate country/background. Some administrators permitted (non-migrant) Australians to join the group, either because their spouse met the criteria (for example, the Australian partner of a Swedish man) or because they expressed an affinity for the culture of the group. As Ana explained:

> A lot of the mums who are not Brazilians have some kind of Brazilian root, either through their husband or they want to know a bit more of the culture, and we want to give a chance to everyone.

In the Brazilian and Swedish groups, where women looking for childcare work were admitted as an exception to the mothers-only rule, nationality became a decisive criterion. Parents sought babysitters who spoke their home language, and a shared country of origin appeared to increase parents' trust, an important consideration when recruiting a carer for one's child. Language and country of origin were deployed in creating a "narrative of sameness" (Seligman 2012, p. 190), which appeared to increase parents' "generalised trust" (Delhey & Newton 2005) and their specific trust in the babysitter's approach to childcare.

In contrast to the relatively untroubled narrative around national identity, the issue of members' place of residence was a source of tension in some groups. Many participants expressed the view that it was important that members lived in the same locality, to facilitate offline encounters and to ensure content shared in the group remained geographically relevant to its members. Some women talked about the importance of having friends who lived close by, meeting up in convenient locations, or being close enough to exchange books or borrow clothes. Women spoke about their range of movement being limited by difficulties accessing public transport with young children and prams, feeling restricted by children's sleep routines, activities, or school hours. Women therefore sought friendship and information from people nearby. Having previously used the British/Irish group to find people to meet up with, Lisa moved out of the area and subsequently found the group less helpful, although she remained a member to give "encouragement" or "advice" to people feeling upset or homesick, maintaining her affective role within the group. Jyoti questioned why many members of the Sydney-based Indian mothers' group lived outside Sydney, remarking "that's a question I've thought of asking admins multiple times." For Jyoti, the questions asked by non-local members distracted from the sense of local relevance, and she contrasted it with her favourite Facebook group for mothers in her local area, which provided useful local information albeit not specifically aimed at migrants. That she considered asking the administrators to explain the presence of non-local people in the group indicates her understanding of the administrators' role in setting and enforcing boundaries.

While members and administrators tended to accept that people might live in a different area of the city, or that they might move within Australia and remain a member, they were less keen to accept people living outside Australia. Indian migrant Usha noted her first request to join had been rejected because her profile information placed her in Dubai. When she explained to the administrator that she was in the process of migrating from Dubai to Australia, her access was granted. Some administrators spoke about balancing the needs of potential migrants using the group to plan, or dream about, migration, with the needs of Australian-based migrants for hyperlocal information and social interaction. Ana recalled a member of the Brazilian group complaining about members who "were not even Brazilians and some were not even in Melbourne." Ana explained her response:

> We are not going to ban someone because they are not here. They might have the intention to come, they need to learn about the country, and it's a good way to get information.

For Ana, facilitating the mobility of her fellow Brazilians is central to the purpose of the group. She advises members on how to facilitate the migration of their parents and works with the Brazilian consulate to welcome new migrants. Ana's community-oriented approach emphasises the importance of the group as a community service. Although her focus is on developing a local community resource, she maintains a diasporic sense of belonging, which includes prospective migrants from Brazil, as well as those who have already made the journey. For others, local relevance and localised diasporic belongings take precedence over transnational connections and loyalties.

In busy social media environments, many users are keen to see only the information most relevant to them, resulting in the development of algorithms as computational solutions to the desire for personalised relevance online. The presence of people with future mobility-focused priorities, rather than current settlement-focused priorities, may frustrate some members' attempts to curate a personalised Facebook experience. Ana's diasporic orientation encompasses the possibility of future migration, echoing Tanja and Jenni's future-focused curation of groups encompassing the possibility of equal parenting. While most administrators drew heavily on quotidian, pragmatic justifications for their boundary work, Ana, Tanja, and Jenni make space for future potentialities.

Constructing the groups as sites of trust

Alongside constructing identities and belongings around the axes of motherhood, national identity, and local residence, the boundary work performed by administrators appears to have another motive: the creation of a community of people who can be trusted. Trust in the context of strangers or acquaintances is referred to as "generalised trust," defined as "the belief that others will not deliberately or knowingly do us harm, if they can avoid it, and will look after our interests, if this is possible" (Delhey & Newton 2005, p. 311). Seligman suggests people construct a "narrative of sameness"– in this case, sameness based on maternity, nationality/ethnicity, and local residence – that brings a sense of confidence that we can predict how another person will behave (2012, p. 190). Delhey and Newton's study concluded that "generalised trust is strongest where we have something in common with others, especially where we are from the same ethnic background" (2005, p. 324). Analysis of the migrant mothers' groups suggests that shared gender, motherhood status, and locality may also be contributory factors to generalised trust.

The groups' boundaries, as upheld by the administrators, provide salient knowledge about the other members, which facilitates "pragmatic trust" (Weigert 2012). Without these mediating boundaries, the groups would constitute a context of complete ignorance, which, as Simmel argues, precludes any rational basis for trust (1950, p. 318, cited in Möllering 2001). Weigert's concept of "pragmatic trust in a world of strangers" is helpful here. The administrators' boundary work enables members to move from "trust-among-strangers," which must be established through "trusting actions," to "in-group trust," which can rely more heavily on assumptions of goodwill and common ground (Weigert 2012, pp. 176–178). In the context of an online group, in which everyone may be a stranger at first, establishing boundaries of common ground appears to increase participants' expectations of trustworthy behaviour. In the context of migration or motherhood, when people may encounter more strangers than usual, and in which they may have greater need to rely on the information, advice, or goodwill of strangers than usual, finding spaces where one can leap into "in-group trust" appears to provide a level of comfort or security that is appealing. The administrators' boundary work enables participants simultaneously to acknowledge that their group consists mostly of strangers and to proceed in "a state of favourable expectations regarding other people's actions and intentions" (Möllering 2001, p. 412). In Grainne's words, "they may be a bunch of strangers, but they're a supportive bunch of strangers online."

Nevertheless, limits and tensions around trust between group members remain. While Winnie trusts the information and advice she receives from Malaysian mothers in the group, she is surprised to observe other members offering to take a new migrant into their home:

Just because they are Malaysian. I wouldn't do that to a stranger! I've got three kids! Invite them to live in my house! Maybe I should, eh? [laughs] Just because they are from Malaysia?!

For Winnie, the "in-group trust" engendered by their common ground as Malaysian mothers may be sufficient for her to trust their information or friendship advances but is not sufficient to overcome her perception of the risk involved in allowing access to her home and children. While migrant mothers are grateful for the support and information provided by relative strangers, albeit strangers with whom they share important common ground and online co-presence, it remains a source of unease. The common ground and "pragmatic trust" created by the administrators' boundary work cannot completely overcome the sense of "strangership" (Horgan 2012) between members.

Distrust congregates in three areas. Firstly, distrust relating to revealing personal information to people who might misuse it, whether that is revealing information about your relationship to your husband's friends, or revealing photographs of your children to people who might use them for nefarious purposes. As Nisha remarks,

I personally wouldn't feel comfortable sharing my kids' photos when I don't know everyone. Or when I don't know whether everyone's a parent or not [...] We take a lot of trouble to screen the requests that come so that we know that 1) they are all in Melbourne, 2) that they are all mums.

Secondly, some participants noted a degree of scepticism towards advice or information offered in the group. Not because of a failure of goodwill on the part of the person offering such information but because of a lack of contextual information relating to their expertise or qualification for offering it. For Diya, while it is "nice" to receive advice from other British mothers, "on the other hand, it's coming from a complete stranger, so it's a bit weird at the same time." Aoife expressed her frustration at people relying on uninformed opinions from group members rather than accessing professional expertise. The third level of distrust relates to a sense of protecting oneself and one's family from "random creeps" (Priya) online or in person. This is what prevents Winnie from taking new migrants into her home – "I've got three kids!"

It is widely acknowledged that trust is culturally specific and measurements of generalised trust vary across nations (see, for example, Delhey & Newton 2005). As this study draws on the experiences of people from a range of countries, I do not attempt to draw concrete conclusions about levels of trust in the groups. The administrators' boundary work can be seen as an attempt to create strategic spaces of trust in which migrant mothers can make pragmatic assumptions of trustworthiness in order to access information and resources that will support them in their role as migrants and mothers. The interaction between the boundary work performed by the administrators and the trust and safety felt by the members indicates the emotional significance of such boundary work and other tasks of curation.

Emotional curation, emotional labour

> It's up to you as a community manager to make sure that everyone is happy, entertained, and achieving their purpose for being on your community.
> (Deborah Ng, *Online community management for dummies*, 2012, p. 19)

In addition to the boundary work performed at the entry and exit points of the group, the administrators also engaged in curation practices within the group, seeking to produce a particular affective environment. While emotional curation is commonly understood as a key part of any community manager's role, as indicated by the quote above from an introductory guide to community management, there is little research on the impact of that emotional curation on either the curators or the community members (De Winter et al. 2017; Jacobson 2017). The argument advanced here is that much of the administrators' emotional curation work seeks to reduce conflict arising from difference, as part of weaving a "narrative of sameness" to increase the trust and empathy shared by group members. It is thus an extension of the boundary work explored in the previous section. Where difference arises, such as with maternal practices, administrators seek to establish a norm of 'compassionate mothering' to minimise the affective disruption in the group. In this context, I propose the term 'compassionate mothering' to refer to compassion between mothers with differing (maternal) practices. It defines relations between mothers, rather than between mother and child. 'Compassionate mothering' stands in contrast to "combative mothering," a term used by Moore and Abetz (2016) to describe media tropes that emphasise "the idea that mothers are in constant competition with one another over parenting choices" (p. 53).

As with the boundary work, the level of emotional curation varied between the groups, with some administrators frequently intervening, usually in the larger groups, and others taking a more 'hands-off' approach. Administrators engaged in both proactive and reactive practices to shape the emotional environment of their group. The proactive practices extended the boundary work of inclusion and exclusion, setting "community norms of practice" (Baym 2015, p. 84) and behavioural boundaries, the transgression of which may lead to censure or expulsion. Administrators set guidelines for permissible content and tone. Sometimes these guidelines were included in the public information about the group, sitting alongside the nomenclature and group description at the entrance to the group. One group urges members to be "pleasant," adding that "any member that doesn't comply will be promptly deleted [smile emoticon]." In their interviews, administrators described role-modelling gentle advice-giving and norms of interaction, sharing their own experiences to encourage others to feel comfortable requesting advice or information and posting light-hearted content to create an atmosphere that is "not intimidating" (Nisha). The administrators' work sets an affective framework in which civility, trust, and empathy are valorised while conflict and incivility are discouraged.

Administrators also engaged in reactive practices, addressing members' undesirable behaviours or encouraging desirable behaviours. For example, administrators described replying to unanswered posts to ensure every "invitation to dialogue" (Pelaprat & Brown 2012) received a response. Administrators intervened in discussions that threatened to bring conflict or incivility into the group, deleted comments or threads, and closed threads to new comments to halt the momentum of an argument. Some administrators contacted members privately to ask them to reconsider their post; others deleted without warning. This emotional curation work involved making judgements about the boundaries between civility and incivility, between "healthy discussion" (Ana) and disruptive difference. Ana had removed ten members from the Brazilian group after a woman called her in tears about comments she had received about breastfeeding:

> It's fine, if someone said, 'Look, I prefer to give formula...' [and someone replied] 'Look, have you considered the benefits of breastfeeding for you and your child?' That's different. But going and saying, 'You are not a mother, you don't deserve to have your child' and swearing at... We thought that got to a very bad point.

In this quote, Ana distinguishes between empathetic difference – "have you considered" – and confrontational difference – "you don't deserve to have your child." While the former implies common maternal ground and an assumption that interlocutors share an interest in achieving the best outcome for the child, the latter casts the formula-feeding mother as a 'bad' mother, as beyond the common ground of 'good' motherhood.

As this example suggests, difference relating to maternal practices – such as infant feeding, co-sleeping, and sleep disturbances – seemed to require particularly careful management. Administrators noted that ostensibly straightforward requests for information and advice could elicit strong, often emotive opinions. Priya described her practice of intervening when she deemed members' advice or comments "insensitive or too direct." Jenni described posting articles in the Swedish parents' group espousing a range of views, to demonstrate her comfort with diversity in maternal practices: "I just think it's really important to have a group and see that people do things differently and we can all be friends."

Conflict among mothers has received attention in public and scholarly discourse, usually focusing on the surveillance and judgement of mothers by other mothers. At its most divisive this has been referred to as "the mommy wars" (Douglas & Michaels 2004; Moore & Abetz 2016). In this study, participants tended to position other mothers in the group as empathetic and supportive, emphasising instead their fear of judgement by non-mothers (men and childless women) to justify the mothers-only space. Nevertheless, administrators' attention to discussions around maternal practices suggests an understanding that these are potential disruptors of their carefully curated space of empathy and trust. This resonates with research that suggests mothers' fear of judgement affects their willingness to express their information needs (Loudon et al. 2016; McKenzie 2002).

This management of difference in relation to maternal practices is common to many online mothers' groups, but the migration context of these groups makes it particularly salient. Women turned to these groups not just for general advice around feeding or sleeping but for advice on how to navigate conflicting advice on these topics, especially where those conflicts appeared to arise from cultural or generational differences. Migration provides a context in which women receive advice from many sources. Some noted that advice from their own mother conflicted with advice from their doctor or maternal peer group. For example, Sunita's mother and her parents-in-law were "pretty upset" that her children had not yet been toilet trained. Many participants spent extended periods of time 'back home' with young children and noted the difference in practices between them and their family members or peers. For example, on a visit to Brazil, Kate objected to her mother's habit of giving juice to Kate's daughter and niece, while her mother objected to Kate's attempts to discipline the children. The participants who had experienced child-raising or pregnancy in more than one country described nuanced differences in medical advice, health systems, and norms around motherhood. Administrators work hard to curate their groups as spaces that can tolerate difference in maternal practices by establishing expectations of empathetic and sensitive interactions, advocating a norm of compassionate mothering to ward off the spectre of "combative mothering" (Moore & Abetz 2016). The administrators' meta-maternal practices establish a norm of compassionate mothering online and constitute a form of digital community mothering.

Curating content to minimise conflict

Unsurprisingly perhaps, given the emphasis on minimising conflict, posts about politics and religion were often deemed inappropriate. In many groups, this occurred without administrative intervention, as members assumed the groups to be apolitical spaces and refrained from posting 'controversial' content of this kind. This is consistent with a view that places motherhood in the private sphere of family, separate from the public sphere of politics and economics (Glenn 1994). Both Brazilian administrators, Kate and Ana, stated that discussions of a political or religious nature were banned, although Maria, a member of the group, recalled discussions about refugees and other news stories. Kate recalled a member's response to the deletion of a religious post, during which the member made public allegations against Kate, causing Kate to fear for her safety. This incident indicates both the potentially disruptive effect of topics like religion and politics, and the potential impact of such conflict on the administrators.

Members of the group for Indian mothers in Sydney reported discussions around politics and current affairs, such as the demonetisation in India, and murder of an Indian bus driver in Brisbane, both of which occurred in October-November 2016, when I conducted most of the interviews with this group. Jyoti cited these two discussions as evidence that she did not fully fit in with the group, noting that this inhibited her from participating in discussions: "I don't [post] because my opinions are not agreed upon by [...] a majority of them." Politics and religion, like the maternal practices discussed above, were seen to be potential disruptors of the group's emotional atmosphere and "narrative of sameness." Discussions around maternal practices were seen to be core to the groups' purpose, so difference in that area required careful management, whereas politics and religion were deemed peripheral and therefore better excluded.

A second area of content curation, which was an issue for administrators in almost every group, was managing posts relating to sales, advertising, and other "business posts." Administrators used a range of strategies including outright prohibition, restricting business posts to specific times or threads, or requiring prior administrator approval. Administrators agreed that regulating business posts was important for maintaining the groups' sense of purpose. Aditi intended to maintain the "essence" of the Indian mothers' group as a "support community" and not "just another buy/sell page." In the South Asian mothers' group, Priya also emphasised support over business: "Because in all fairness, this is a support group, so if you want to do business, we do every Tuesday for business. But if you think Saturday is a Tuesday and if you post, that's not ok." Managing business posts was, as Priya's tone indicates, a source of frustration for many administrators and could cause conflict with members. The conflict was deemed worthwhile to maintain the integrity of the group. As Ana explained: "we've created the group with one intention, and we want that to continue. If the rules are not followed, we have no other choice. We have a lot of conflicts over that."

Some administrators were more supportive of transactional posts, noting that women used the groups to offer migrant-specific services to members who might find them difficult to source elsewhere, such as traditional postnatal massage, catering, and handmade or imported clothing. In turn, those mostly small-scale services provided opportunities for income generation among women who might otherwise struggle. Karen, the administrator of the Singaporean mothers' group, opined, "it's good for the mums if they want to advertise their business, especially if there are good things to share, but [...] if you just join for the sake of advertising, then I say no, I will block you or I will delete the post." For Karen, motives are crucial. It is appropriate for a 'genuine' member to leverage their network to promote their business. But somebody who joins with the sole purpose of promoting their business and shows no interest in engaging in friendship, support, or information exchange is deemed to be a 'bad maternal digital citizen' and is expelled. The migrant maternal groups may include transactional and promotional interactions as by-products of the social, informational, and emotional interactions, but they must not overshadow the primary purpose of the group.

Curating opportunities for offline social interaction

Most administrators took on the role of facilitating opportunities for social interaction beyond the digital space of the groups. Only two administrators had never organised an offline meeting, and one of those (Sherry) had created an online file of members' details to facilitate independent meet-ups. Members of the British/ Irish group asked Rebecca to arrange meet-ups, and she did so. For Rebecca, this was an unexpected addition to her role, indicating that the role of these 'accidental community managers' may be shaped by expectations on both sides.

Offline meet-ups were primarily arranged to facilitate social interaction between mothers, with secondary motivations around children's social and/or linguistic development, and cultural maintenance. In terms of participants, events fell into three categories: mothers and children; mothers only; and family events. Events for mothers and children included casual meet-ups in parks or cafes, or more organised 'playgroup' activities. Playgroups involved additional labour: finding a venue, organising activities, marketing and promotion, and in some cases employing an educator to lead the group. Events exclusively for mothers primarily involved dinners in a local restaurant and, less commonly, cinema trips and visits to tourist attractions. Family events took place at weekends, to enable spouses to attend, and mostly involved picnics or cultural festivities. The offline meet-ups reflected the changing needs of the members. Groups that had been formed around mothers on maternity leave, with regular meet-ups in parks and cafes, found such meet-ups became less frequent as members returned to work and children became more active and enrolled in organised activities. Evening activities tended to be less affected by these changes, as mothers' need for social interaction continued to be salient beyond the early months of motherhood.

As with all elements of the administrators' role, facilitating these offline events involved unpaid labour. Unlike other tasks, which could be completed during the day, on their phone, fitting between other family and work responsibilities, weekend events required negotiation with their spouses, who were often reluctant to participate. While her husband preferred to prioritise time as a family, Maria expressed a sense of duty to assist her fellow Spanish-speaking migrants: "I believe that we have to help. We have had a lot of support from different people, and I think we need to do it." Sabina noted that she had "dragged" her husband to events to "encourage the dads to come" but admitted "he really didn't want to come." This gendered, unpaid, labour is the focus of the next section.

Conceptualising the role of the administrators

The final sections of this chapter explore the gendered and maternal labour undertaken by the administrators, drawing on concepts like "digital housewives" (Jarrett 2016) and "community mothers" (Collins 1991, 1994; Edwards 2000; hooks 1984; O'Reilly 2004) to suggest they may be engaged *in meta-maternal practices* that constitute a kind of *digital community mothering*.

From accidental community management to maternal leadership

None of the women had anticipated when starting the group that their role might grow into one that required skilled interpersonal communication and near-constant vigilance. The 'accidental community manager' role brought hard work and rewards. While the administrators of smaller, or less active, groups described their role with more nonchalance, others described a deep sense of responsibility to their group. With the volume of posts, the round-the-clock vigilance required, and the expectations from members to explain administrative decisions, Aditi described her admin role as "exhausting." She felt a strong sense of obligation to the group, and the need to continuously monitor the group encroached on her family life. Administrators of larger groups, or those who took a more interventionist approach, were more likely to describe their role as exhausting or time-consuming, particularly if they received little positive feedback from members, or encountered pressure from their partner due to the time they devoted to it. At times of personal crisis, managing the group took an additional toll, particularly the emotionally fraught moderation of disputes. Ana noted that her interventionist approach created conflict with members as the imbalance of power within this peer-led community becomes manifest: "for some reason, they think they have the right to post whatever they want!" Ana expressed a tension between administrators' responsibility to curate the content and conversation to maintain the peer support community, and their desire not to be seen as "dictators of the group."

Nevertheless, Ana, like many of the administrators, expressed a sense of pride and achievement. Aditi pronounced herself "very proud, to tell you the truth. We didn't expect it to be so big, but the fact that it's becoming big, I'm proud of it." For Yasmin: "It's one of my achievements in life so far," and the group is "a feather in my cap" for Nisha. Karen reflected with satisfaction on her role in facilitating connections between Singaporean mothers:

> I am very happy when I hear people telling me, 'Before this group, before I know you, I don't know any Singaporean. I have been here for 18 years, but I don't know any other Singaporean that is here.' [...] I'm happy for them that through this link, through my link, they managed to meet other friends.

Both the pride and vulnerability expressed by Ana and the other administrators arose from the visibility of their leadership role in their online maternal communities, which brought increased social connections as well as responsibilities.

Managing the groups has brought administrators reciprocal relationships, vicarious pleasure at observing emerging relationships between members, and also increased visibility within their migrant maternal community and beyond. In contrast to the loneliness and isolation Aditi felt when she had her first child in Sydney, she is now "much more social." She has many friends and acquaintances to meet up with, and the other administrators of her group have "become good friends." Kate, too, has met a wide range of people through her role, which has made her feel "popular" and "important," especially when people express their gratitude for the group. Through their role, the administrators have re-established their social status and social networks, which were disrupted when they left their home country and again when they became mothers. Counteracting the individualisation and privatisation of motherhood, or the confinement of motherhood to a 'private sphere,' the administrators have brought motherhood into this semi-public space, emphasising the importance of relationships between mothers. Mothers become visible to each other, and through the leadership of these groups, the administrators gain the visibility of a public role:

> People will just randomly come up to me and say, 'Are you Priya from [group]?' [...] I don't mean to sound like I have a celebrity status, but most people would know me or the other two [admins].

The visibility of this role suggests that the administrators are engaged in a kind of maternal leadership or 'meta maternal' role. Drawing on the concept of online "micro-celebrities," a term proposed by Marwick (2013) to describe people who become famous to a niche group of people via social media, I suggest that some of the administrators have become 'accidental micro-celebrities' as a corollary of their role as 'accidental community managers.' They become well-known within their niche community of migrant mothers, as their name, profile, and interactions bring recognition online that translates into recognition in the streets, shops, and parks.

Unlike the professional community managers interviewed by Jacobson (2017), these 'accidental community managers' did not engage in "identity curation" or "personal branding," but their role in curating the communities led them to become identified with the group, and visible within it. This visibility spilled over into other areas, such as their workplace, or their husband's workplace. Nisha recalled two occasions when her husband had been approached in his workplace by members of the group, leading him to declare, "People know you more than they know me!" This public recognition of her work has increased his estimation of it, and she says he now recommends it to women he encounters. For Nisha, who has spent years following her husband's work across three continents, taking temporary, often unpaid work and raising two small children, this public and spousal recognition of her community work is significant. By contrast, Aditi's husband found it "intimidating" to be approached by group members in his workplace. The intrusion of these "intimate mothering publics" (Johnson 2015) into the workplace is unsettling, troubling the binary that assigns motherhood to the domestic, private sphere. Their administrator role "stretches" their motherhood beyond domestic spaces, into online social spaces, and offline workplaces (Longhurst 2013).

This 'accidental micro-celebrity' status may bring increased social status and increased social connections and self-esteem, but the increased visibility may also bring vulnerability to judgement or even fears for personal safety. Priya joked that members tended to approach her just as she was wrangling her "misbehaving" children – "the most embarrassing times" – while Jenni said her role in the group made her reluctant to ask for advice about social welfare payments. In a context in which mothers are hyperaware of societal surveillance and judgement, accepting a 'meta-maternal' role, in which they feel a responsibility to embody an ideal of knowledgeable information exchange and compassionate mothering, increases the administrators' exposure to potential judgement.

Digital housewives and digital community mothers

Feminist scholars of digital media have drawn parallels between the unpaid "consumer labour" undertaken by users of participative internet sites and the unpaid domestic labour undertaken, traditionally and still most commonly, by women. Using a Marxist feminist analysis, Jarrett introduces the figure of the "Digital Housewife":

> Like housewives, consumers receive little or no direct financial compensation for their contributions to the revenue-generating mechanisms of digital media sites so that all of their labour produces surplus-value for the website provider.
>
> (2016, p. 11)

Commercially run websites like Facebook rely on consumers to generate content, to generate data to be sold to advertisers, to consume that advertising, and "to manage and maintain the symbolic and affective dimensions of their platforms," including "policing other users" (Jarrett 2016, p. 79). Through this lens, all interactions by both administrators and members can be viewed as capital creation for the owners of Facebook. Jarrett argues that such consumer labour, while inherently exploitative, may be experienced as creative or empowering: "Like domestic work, consumer labour is both exploited and a site that serves myriad other socially meaningful functions." While Jarrett's argument treats consumer labourers as gender-neutral, other scholars have linked the social, affective, and relational labour performed by women online to "women's work" more broadly. Jacobson (2017) describes online community management as "the newest pink collar job" being gendered as naturally more suitable for women, involving care and relational work, and undervalued in comparison to masculine-coded work (p. 97). De Winter et al. (2017) agree that community management is a "feminized profession" defined by "communication, care, and emotional labor" (p. 40).

In terms of unwaged work, as noted above, scholars have argued for women's online affective and relational labour to be seen as an extension of their offline labour in these areas (Ouellette & Wilson 2011; Portwood-Stacer 2014). Bringing these analyses together with a Marxist narrative, Arcy (2016) argues that "these practices are indissociable from traditional sexual division of labor whereby capital accumulation depends upon women's unpaid labor" (p. 366). From the perspective of their lived experience, the migrant mothers in this study use the groups to carry out their responsibilities for their family's affective settlement after migration. Furthermore, the administrators' role has extended beyond this family-centred responsibility into a kind of meta-responsibility: a responsibility for the affective settlement of other people's families.

Drawing on a concept from Black feminist scholarship, I argue that this 'meta-maternal' role is a kind of digital "community mothering" (Collins 1991, 2000a; Edwards 2000; Lawson 2000), in which women take on responsibility for the wellbeing of children, mothers, and families in their community. As this Black feminist scholarship theorises from a specific African American context, in which community mothering has been a strategy for community survival, I use this term with some caution to refer to maternal practices that extend beyond one's own children. Collins describes "women-centered networks of bloodmothers and othermothers" in which relatives and neighbours provide care to children and support to mothers, with the understanding that communities, not just individual mothers, are responsible for the children of the community (2000b, p. 178). Edwards (2000) notes that in African American communities, community mothering may involve advocating for the needs of the community, providing "moral mothering" for children in the community, and spearheading the creation of institutions to address the needs of the community, particularly in the areas of health and education. Thus, African American community mothering can refer to a maternal role in relation to children other than one's own, or to a meta-maternal activist role on behalf of the whole community.

Conclusion

Maternal metaphors are common in discussions of professional community management and in the accounts given by the administrators in this study. As with motherhood, carework, and other social reproductive labour, stereotypes of women's natural capacity for nurture and empathy are used to devalue their work in community management (Jacobson 2017). Many of the administrators noted that their husbands did not value their work with the group. Nisha's husband characterised her work as "just wasting more time on Facebook" (her words) until his co-workers' validation of its value caused him to reconsider.

In this chapter, I have proposed the term 'meta-maternal practices' to conceptualise the type of labour deployed by the administrators to manage the groups. These practices include establishing and maintaining boundaries and behaviours through role-modelling, empathetic interventions and compassionate discipline, and nurturing relationships between the members. They are the metaphorical mothers of their online community. I have extended this idea by drawing on concepts of "community mothering" from Black feminist thought, which emphasise an "ethic of care" that extends beyond the needs of one's own children (Collins 1991). While the administrators did not engage in the kind of political and social activism that is often associated with "community mothering" in African American communities, their meta-maternal practices constitute a form of maternally based community service and maternal community-building in migration. Ana's administrator role is part of a lifetime of community service: "I've grown up like that, I've always been community, [...] since I was 8 years old, I was serving soup in a church, so I was always involved with that, so I can't see myself not doing." Ana uses this community service narrative to justify her involvement to her husband, who, although supportive, does not share her dedication to community service and has suggested she dedicate less time to the group.

I draw on concepts of community mothering to conceptualise the administrators' maternal role in the online communities, creating and caring for the groups and moulding behaviours within the groups. In this sense, they are 'mothers' of their digital communities. The administrators also provide care and support for other mothers in their community, whether by providing the group as a space in which they can seek support and friendship, by encouraging compassion between mothers, or by coordinating hands-on support for mothers in their community. The context in which this meta-mothering occurs is one in which mothers' social infrastructure and/or extended family networks have often been disrupted by migration. In a migrant context, these digital community mothers facilitate the rebuilding of that social infrastructure; create ways for migrant mothers to exchange information, friendship and support; and organise formal and informal opportunities for community events and cultural transmission, such as playgroups and parties.

In the context of migration, Manohar argues, women build community to perform two migration-specific forms of carework: defining and generating new senses of belonging for their family, and providing an alternative to the "extended kin safety network" they have lost through migration (2013, p. 30). Here, the administrators' digital nurturing provides an online community infrastructure that allows other migrant mothers to fulfil their gendered affective settlement responsibilities to their family. It creates a space where mothers can generate new senses of belonging based on shared migrant maternal experiences and can support each other in their maternal cultural maintenance role. The administrators' "community mothering" supports the children of their community by helping women to fulfil their various maternal roles. In addition, it supports women to meet their own need for friendship and social interaction and to become an affective resource for each other. The next chapter will explore how migrant mothers imagine themselves within local, national, and diasporic maternal communities and within personal maternal narratives that may have been disrupted by migration.

Note

1 More recently, most administrators have gained access to Facebook functionality that allows them to set questions for all potential members to answer as part of the approval process. At the time of interviewing, however, none of the administrators had access to this functionality.

References

Arcy, J. (2016). Emotion work: Considering gender in digital labor. *Feminist Media Studies*, 16(2), 365–368. doi:10.1080/14680777.2016.1138609.

Australian Community Managers (ACM). (2019). Australian Community Managers (ACM) career survey. Retrieved from https://www.australiancommunitymanagers. com.au/research.

Bareither, C. (2019). Doing emotion through digital media: An ethnographic perspective on media practices and emotional affordances. *Ethnologia Europaea*, 49(1). doi:10.16995/ee.822.

Baym, N. K. (2015). *Personal connections in the digital age* (2nd ed.). Cambridge, UK: Polity Press.

Bell, D. (2007). Webs as pegs. In D. Bell, & B. M. Kennedy (Eds.), *The cybercultures reader* (2nd ed., pp. 254–263). New York; London: Routledge.

Bernal, V. (2014). *Nation as network: Diaspora, cyberspace, and citizenship*. Chicago: The University of Chicago Press.

Bogle, A. (2018). How community management and policing internet trolls became women's work. *ABC News Online*. Retrieved from https://www.abc.net.au/news/sci ence/2018-05-31/how-policing-internet-trolls-became-womens-work/9808634.

Bos, N., Olson, J., Gergle, D., Olson, G., & Wright, Z. (2002). *Effects of four computer-mediated communications channels on trust development*. Paper presented at the Proceedings of the SIGCHI Conference on Human Factors in Computing Systems. Minneapolis, Minnesota, USA.

Cohen, A. P. (1985). *The symbolic construction of community*. Chichester; London; New York: E. Horwood.

Collins, P. H. (1991). The meaning of motherhood in Black culture and Black mother-daughter relationships. In P. Bell-Scott (Ed.), *Double stitch: Black women write about mothers & daughters*. Boston: Beacon Press.

Collins, P. H. (1994). Shifting the center: Race, class, and feminist theorizing about motherhood. In E. N. Glenn, G. Chang, & L. R. Forcey (Eds.), *Mothering: ideology, experience, and agency*. NY/London: Routledge.

Collins, P. H. (2000a). *Black feminist thought: Knowledge, consciousness, and the politics of empowerment*. Revised 10th anniversary ed. Routledge.

Collins, P. H. (2000b). Black women and motherhood. In *Black feminist thought* (pp. 173–199). Revised 10th anniversary ed. Routledge.

Delhey, J., & Newton, K. (2005). Predicting cross-national levels of social trust: Global pattern or Nordic exceptionalism? *European Sociological Review*, 21(4), 311–327. doi:10.1093/esr/jci022.

De Winter, J., Kocurek, C. A., & Vie, S. (2017). Managing community managers: Social labor, feminized skills, and professionalization. *Communication Design Quarterly Review*, 4(4), 36–45. doi:10.1145/3071088.3071092.

Douglas, S. J., & Michaels, M. W. (2004). *The mommy myth: The idealization of motherhood and how it has undermined all women.* Free Press.

Duffy, B. E., & Schwartz, B. (2018). Digital "women's work?": Job recruitment ads and the feminization of social media employment. *New Media & Society,* 20(8), 2972–2989. doi:10.1177/1461444817738237.

Edwards, A. E. (2000). Community mothering: The relationship between mothering and the community work of Black women. *Journal of the Motherhood Initiative for Research and Community Involvement,* 2(2), 87–100.

Feng, J., Lazar, J., & Preece, J. (2004). Empathy and online interpersonal trust: A fragile relationship. *Behaviour & Information Technology,* 23(2), 97–106. doi:10.1080/01449290310001659240.

Fox, B. (2009). *When couples become parents: The creation of gender in the transition to parenthood.* Toronto: University of Toronto Press.

Fuchs, C. (2014). *Social media: A critical introduction.* London: SAGE. doi:10.4135/9781446270066.

Glenn, E. N. (1994). Social constructions of mothering: A thematic overview. In E. N. Glenn, G. Chang, & L. R. Forcey (Eds.), *Mothering: Ideology, experience, and agency* (pp. 1–29). New York: Routledge.

Henderson, S., & Gilding, M. (2004). 'I've never clicked this much with anyone in my life': Trust and hyperpersonal communication in online friendships. *New Media and Society,* 6(4), 487–506. doi:10.1177/146144804044331.

hooks, b. (1984). *Feminist theory: From margin to center.* Cambridge, MA: South End Press.

Horgan, M. (2012). Strangers and strangership. *Journal of Intercultural Studies,* 33(6), 607–622. doi:10.1080/07256868.2012.735110.

Jacobson, J. (2017). "I work in social": Community managers and personal branding in social media (PhD). University of Toronto. Retrieved from http://hdl.handle.net/1807/80920.

Jarrett, K. (2016). *Feminism, labour and digital media: The digital housewife.* New York: Routledge.

Johnson, S. (2015). 'Intimate mothering publics': Comparing face-to-face support groups and internet use for women seeking information and advice in the transition to first-time motherhood. *Culture, Health & Sexuality,* 17(2), 237–251. doi:10.1080/13691058.2014.968807.

Kvist, E., & Peterson, E. (2010). What has gender equality got to do with it? An analysis of policy debates surrounding domestic services in the welfare states of Spain and Sweden. *NORA - Nordic Journal of Feminist and Gender Research,* 18(3), 185–203. doi:10.1080/08038740.2010.498326.

Lawson, E. (2000). Black women's mothering in a historical and contemporary perspective: Understanding the past, forging the future. *Journal of the Motherhood Initiative for Research and Community Involvement,* 2(2), 21–30.

Lohan, M. (2000). Constructive tensions in feminist technology studies. *Social Studies of Science,* 30(6), 895–916.

Longhurst, R. (2013). Stretching mothering: Gender, space and information communication technologies. *Hagar,* 11(1), 121–138.

Loudon, K., Buchanan, S., & Ruthven, I. (2016). The everyday life information seeking behaviours of first-time mothers. *Journal of Documentation,* 72(1), 24–46. doi:10.1108/JD-06-2014-0080.

Manohar, N. N. (2013). Support networks, ethnic spaces, and fictive kin: Indian immigrant women constructing community in the United States. *AAPI Nexus: Policy, Practice and Community*, 11(1–2),25–55. doi:10.17953/appc.11.1-2.t81xj18224638u44.

Marwick, A. E. (2013). *Status update: Celebrity, publicity, and branding in the social media age.* Yale University Press.

McKenzie, P. J. (2002). Communication barriers and information-seeking counterstrategies in accounts of practitioner-patient encounters. *Library and Information Science Research*, 24(1), 31–47. doi:10.1016/S0740-8188(01)00103-7.

McMillan, D. W., & Chavis, D. M. (1986). Sense of community: A definition and theory. *Journal of Community Psychology*, 14(1), 6–23. doi:10.1002/1520-6629 (198601)14:1-6:AID-JCOP2290140103-3.0.CO;2-I.

Möllering, G. (2001). The nature of trust: From Georg Simmel to a theory of expectation, interpretation and suspension. *Sociology*, 35(2), 403–420. doi:10.1017/S0038038501000 190.

Moore, J., & Abetz, J. (2016). "Uh oh. Cue the [new] mommy wars": The ideology of combative mothering in popular U.S. newspaper articles about attachment parenting. *Southern Communication Journal*, 81(1), 49–62. doi:10.1080/1041794X.2015.1076026.

Ng, D. (2012). *Online community management for dummies.* Hoboken, NJ: Wiley.

O'Reilly, A. (2004). *Toni Morrison and motherhood: A politics of the heart.* Albany: State University of New York Press.

Ouellette, L., & Wilson, J. (2011). Women's work. *Cultural Studies*, 25(4/5), 548–565. doi:10.1080/09502386.2011.600546.

Paech, V. (2012). The inevitable exile: A missing link in online community discourse. In T. Brabazon (Ed.), *Digital dialogues and community 2.0: After avatars, trolls and puppets* (pp. 11–41). Elsevier.

Pelaprat, E., & Brown, B. (2012). Reciprocity: Understanding online social relations. *First Monday*, 17(10). doi:10.5210/fm.v17i10.3324.

Pirolli, P. (2009). *An elementary social information foraging model.* Paper presented at the Proceedings of the SIGCHI Conference on Human Factors in Computing Systems.

Portwood-Stacer, L. (2014). Care work and the stakes of social media refusal. *New Criticals.* Retrieved from http://www.newcriticals.com/care-work-and-the-stakes-of-social-media-refusal/print.

Ruddick, S. (1980). Maternal thinking. *Feminist Studies*, 6(2), 342–367. doi:10.2307/ 3177749.

Seligman, A. B. (2012). Trust, tolerance and the challenge of difference. In R. M. Marsh, & M. S. Sasaki (Eds.), *Trust: Comparative perspectives* (pp. 189–208). Leiden: Brill.

Smart, C. (1996). Deconstructing motherhood. In E. B. Silva (Ed.), *Good enough mothering?* (pp. 45–65). London: Routledge.

Suwada, K. (2017). *Men, fathering and the gender trap: Sweden and Poland Compared.* Springer International Publishing. doi:10.1007/978-3-319-47782-4.

Weigert, A. J. (2012). Pragmatic trust in a world of strangers: Trustworthy actions. In R. M. Marsh, & M. S. Sasaki (Eds.), *Trust: Comparative perspectives* (pp. 173–188). Leiden: Brill.

5 Connected maternal migrants and imagined maternal communities

Introduction

Maria

Maria is a Colombian 39-year-old mother of two and runs the group for Spanish-speaking mothers in Melbourne. She met her Brazilian husband in Australia when they were both on student visas. Maria struggled with becoming a mother away from home, contrasting it with the family and community support she imagines she would have had in Colombia. She didn't feel able to confide in her mother about her worries around pregnancy, birth, and child-raising. Now her children are older (5 and 2), she video calls her mother and involves her in their daily routine: "I put her on and […] I'm doing lunch boxes and doing this and doing that, and she's just, as if she were in there and I'm just talking and running from one side to the other and the kids as well … not like a phone call… she's just in there, present in there, and she just sees what happens."

As a new mother, Maria wrestled with conflicting advice from healthcare professionals, her mother and mother-in-law, her state-run mothers' group, and the Australian/US baby books she read. She remembers, "in Colombia you put a lot of clothing on baby. You keep them extremely warm, and here is like you don't cover the babies at all! So normally my mothers' group used to tell me, you put a lot of clothing on your baby, and I was like 'argh, just let me alone! It's the way I do it.' When her daughter was six months' old, Maria met the woman who created the Spanish-speaking mothers group through their local health centre. They became close friends and Maria took over running the group when her friend moved to Sydney.

Maria has been a bit disappointed in the Facebook group, although she notes that the spin-off WhatsApp group seems to be more active, driven by close personal connections and quick responses to questions. She compares it to the Brazilian mothers' group, of which she is also a member, and suggests the Spanish-speaking group might be hindered by the lack of a common origin or identity. While she doesn't feel she gets much personal benefit out of the group anymore, she is committed to her role in it, viewing it as a kind of community service.

In Chapter 2, I showed how national identity acts as a key organising principle for the online migrant maternal groups and can overlap or intersect with ethnic, linguistic, or regional identities. In this chapter, national identity is conceived as a collection of historical practices, a spatially based community, and a socially constructed – and imagined – solidarity. Migrant mothers carry their connections to these practices, community, and solidarity with them. Those who become mothers in migration may find those attachments are activated, or re-activated, by their new maternal role. Drawing on Diminescu's concept of "connected migrants" (2008), I suggest they are *connected maternal migrants*: connected contemporaneously to their networks of friends and family, as Diminescu argues, and also connected across space and time to their imagined maternal communities. Their connections to those imagined communities, like their connections to their digitally enabled networks of family and friends, may be disrupted, re-imagined, or jeopardised by the process of migration.

Motherhood scholars have demonstrated the many ways in which motherhood is contextual, contingent, and shaped by gender ideologies and "good mother" discourses (for example, Collins 2000; Goodwin & Huppatz 2010; Thurer 1995 [1994]). Scholars of migrant motherhood have shown how the experience of migration can change notions of "good motherhood" and maternal practices, whether migration involves mothers being apart from their children (Hondagneu-Sotelo & Avila 1997; Madianou 2012; Meyers & Rugunanan 2020) or being co-located with their children in a migrant context (Ho 2006; Liamputtong 2006; Manohar 2013a; Manohar & Busse-Cárdenas 2011; Utomo 2014; Ziaian 2000). This chapter is framed by an understanding that migrant mothering of co-located children can involve "complex reinventions of everyday practices to produce a sense of identity and belonging that is never fixed and taken for granted" (Gedalof 2009, p. 89). One example of this reinvention of everyday practice is the ethnic socialisation of children, undertaken by mothers in their role as keepers of culture and described by Manohar as "mothering for ethnicity" (Manohar 2013a). It is important to note that all families, migrant and non-migrant, in both marginalised and dominant groups, attempt to instil a sense of ethnic-cultural identity. While non-migrant families from culturally dominant groups may do this largely unconsciously, leaning on mainstream media representations, institutions, and discourse, migrant and marginalised families must do this explicitly and intentionally, drawing on personal, familial, and national narratives (Keller 2010). While this chapter draws on Manohar's concept of "mothering for ethnicity," it places it within a broader perspective, which explores the role of personal narratives and imagined maternal communities in migrant mothers' approaches to motherhood. Central to the analysis is Manohar's finding that "women are not passive performers of cultural norms regarding motherhood, but active creators of it" (2013a, p. 180).

In addition to migration and mothering scholarship, this chapter draws on Kanno and Norton's re-working of the concept of "imagined communities," proposed by Benedict Anderson to conceptualise a sense of belonging in nation-states, which transcends tangible and immediate personal connections (Anderson 2006 [1983]; Kanno & Norton 2003). Kanno and Norton re-work the notion of imagined communities to provide "a theoretical framework for the exploration of creativity, hope, and desire in identity construction" (2003, p. 248). They argue that the community (or communities) people imagine themselves to belong to influences their choices and can (re)frame their interpretation of their action. Imagined communities, they suggest, "expand our range of possible selves" (2003, p. 246). Although imagination implies hope and possibility, Kanno and Norton also note that the imaginary that is available to a person or group may be limited by "social ideologies and hegemonies" (p. 247).

As well as being central to identity and emotion, the imagination can also be a decision-making tool or coping mechanism for migrants, as Adams (2004) shows in her study of cross-national couples' discussions about where they should live. In a context dominated by Western dualism, in which 'reality' and 'rationality' are accorded more validity than imagination or emotion, framing another person's imaginings as "mere fantasy" serves to undermine them. Adams suggests that a person with less power may be more likely to have their imagination dismissed in this way, and more likely to use imagination as a "refuge" to assuage the sadness they feel about a situation they cannot change (pp. 289–290). In relation to motherhood, Baraitser has suggested that motherhood "creates a commons that is the endurance of communality across time" (2012, p. 121). For Baraitser, motherhood generates "the potential for new and unexpected social bonds" that are not limited to the present moment or immediate locality. Drawing these concepts together, I explore how migrant mothers imagine themselves within local, national, and diasporic maternal communities, how their attachment to these maternal communities may be experienced as "new and unexpected," how these imagined connections can be deployed as decision-making tools or coping mechanisms, and how they relate to identity construction, hope, and desire. The migrant maternal imaginary, as it is used in this chapter, is not so much a means by which specific national or ethnic models of motherhood are (re)produced; rather, it is a framework for thinking about the experiential and abstract resources on which mothers draw as they try to make sense of their identity as a mother 'away from home' and try to navigate what it means to be a good mother in this context.

As women move into motherhood as migrants, or move into migration as mothers, a powerful but mostly unexamined narrative surfaces and is challenged by the new context. This narrative is individual, relating to childhood memories and self-identity, and is imbued with hopes for their own future. It is also relational and familial, formed through memories, family stories, interactions with family members, with her partner, with her baby, and it shapes her hopes for her children's future. The narrative also is social and cultural, shaped by popular discourses and interactions with institutions and other mothers, and framed by state legislation and national or ethnic identities. It is a narrative of what she knows about motherhood, what she understands about herself and her nation or culture, what it means to be a German mother, an Indian mother, or a Brazilian mother, how her child's life should unfold and her role in that process. In Maria's words, "it's all the culture, like the things that you have seen that are done, and what you heard, that they need to be done." Migration challenges the cohesion of that narrative. This challenge may be experienced as rupture, as conflict, as autonomy, as loss. This chapter examines women's responses to the challenge presented to their maternal narrative. In migration, maternal practices become a site of increased intentionality, charged with meaning about identity, connection, and hope. In discussing their decision-making and emotions around maternal practices, the migrant mothers in this study appeared to draw on imagined communities of maternal practice and identity, which shaped their choices and how they framed them.

In the rest of the chapter, I analyse how these maternal narratives become activated as women move into migrant motherhood and imagine themselves as inside, outside, or between imagined maternal communities, which are underpinned by different values and logics. For example, I explore how the Swedish mothers drew on values of gender equality, which they defined as national values, to explain their attachment to gender-equal or shared parenting. I analyse how everyday decisions about maternal practices, such as swaddling or discipline, are made in relation to an imagined maternal community, leading to comments such as "we don't swaddle babies in Germany."

There is an important temporal element to these imagined communities. Women draw on individual narratives based on memories of their own childhood, of being mothered, to anchor themselves within their imagined maternal community. Past and present policies shape personal experiences, and women draw on historical and national specificities to contextualise their own maternal practices. The imagined communities also have a future into which women project themselves and their children. Migration troubles the temporal continuity of women's maternal narratives, introducing rupture and discontinuity. In response, women choose to draw on attachments and connections to frame, understand, and reconcile themselves to these challenges. The migrant maternal online communities are sites in which these connections are forged. While other attachments and networks remain salient, I suggest the migrant maternal online communities constitute a metonymic representation of their diasporic maternal community.

Activating imagined migrant maternal communities

Women who became mothers some years after their migration to Australia described how motherhood sparked an increased interest in their national or ethnic attachments, particularly in relation to their new maternal role. Before becoming a mother, Stefanie had few German friends in Australia. Living in Australia for over a decade before having her son, married to an Australian man, Stefanie had felt no need to seek out other German migrants. Indeed, she continued to be sceptical about how much common ground she had with most German migrants, whom she described in our interview as arrogant, transient, querulous, and unwilling to adapt to Australian life. Stefanie did not imagine herself as part of a community of German migrants in Australia, but once she became a mother, she began to identify with an imagined community of German mothers. This was reflected in how she thought and spoke about motherhood, and in the choices she made about maternal practices and the people she surrounded herself with. In explaining why the friends she has made since becoming a mother have mostly been German, Stefanie contends, "we raise our children fundamentally different to a lot of Australian people." She explains this difference with reference to their own childhoods: "I think they grow up very differently to the way I've grown up, so I wouldn't watch much TV, I wouldn't watch any American TV." This difference then manifests in the way Stefanie's son plays:

> I think, just from a toys perspective, so, yes, I know a lot of Australians do play with the same toys, but a lot of Australians always have these electronic telephones, and it doesn't interest him. So he just, he plays very differently, and I think a lot of the German girls do the same, so, so…

Stefanie's narrative makes clear that "mothering for ethnicity" is not simply about passing down knowledge or values to the child but also about enacting a mode of mothering that reflects and produces her sense of being a mother from a particular place and who has been formed by her own experiences of childhood. Stefanie positions herself within an imagined German maternal community, the members of which raise their children in a way that is distinct from the dominant maternal practices in Australia. To support her in maintaining these practices and this sense of herself as a 'good German mother in diaspora,' Stefanie has drawn around her a local network of German mothers, centred on the German mothers' Facebook group. This German maternal identity, practice, and community help to produce a sense of her son as a German child who "plays very differently" from the Australian children around him. Stefanie's sense of this difference produces a desire for support and validation from German maternal peers.

Kavita, a British migrant with Indian heritage, had lived in Australia for nearly a decade before becoming a mother. Her experience illustrates how migrants position themselves in relation to different imagined communities, and how motherhood shifts that positioning, activating attachments which had been less salient. When she and her husband, also a British migrant with Indian heritage, settled together in Sydney, they chose to live in Sydney's eastern suburbs, an area she identifies as suitable for "young professionals" in contrast to Sydney's western suburbs, where they might have found a more established Indian community. "Reasonably solid" in their British-Indian identities, and imagining themselves as part of a mobile, middle-class migrant community, they had felt little need to forge links with Indian communities in Sydney beyond a desire to locate food and ingredients that they were used to having easy access to in the UK.

Pregnancy activated a familial and cultural narrative in which Kavita would be nurtured by female relatives in pregnancy and early motherhood. Kavita's geographically distant female-centred family network, which emphasised Indian prenatal and postnatal rituals and traditions, became more significant, but distance prevented them from actively cooking and caring for her. Kavita instead gathered recipes from her older female relatives and prepared them herself:

> I got the recipes from my mum, and my mother in law, and my aunts, all that age of women in our family, and I said we need these because there's not always going to be someone who can do these things for us. We're going to have to do them for ourselves. So I made a lot of these things for me; I actually made a semolina pudding that's really nourishing when I was in pre-labour, so it was ready for when I came home.

In caring for herself in this way, Kavita was not just connecting to her heritage; she was drawing on an imagined Indian maternal community that takes prenatal and postnatal care of mothers seriously, in a way Kavita suggested was less common in "our Western society." Had Kavita been a member of an Indian mothers' online group when she became a mother, she could have taken advantage of the services she sees offered through the group:

> There's a lot of first-generation women that have come over that will cook, so you can get this tiffin service where someone will cook for you for a week and bring food over. I might not have done that, but I might have asked somebody to bring me some of those postnatal foods and drinks over.

Moving into motherhood activated Kavita's desire for a locally based Indian maternal community to support her maternal project of raising her daughter with sufficient understanding of her Indian heritage. In fact, it was her daughter's first Diwali that inspired Kavita to look online for Indian community groups. She recalled, "I posted on every page I knew to see if there were any Indian mums out there, you know, what do they do for Diwali, where could we go." For Kavita, good mothering involves not just teaching her daughter about Indian languages, clothing, festivals, and music. It also involves making a place for her daughter, and their heritage, in their local community. She feels a particular responsibility because their decision to live away from established Indian communities in Sydney means "she's not around many brown faces at the moment":

> I'm not happy about that. I mean, I did make the conscious decision to live in [Sydney's eastern suburbs], but not at the expense of my daughter being able to … […] I wonder if she'll think, am I different and are there other people like me? I need to make sure that she's around those other people like her.

She noted that her own identity as a "person of colour" had not been on her "radar" for many years but that becoming a mother had brought it back to her attention.

Like Stefanie, Kavita drew on her childhood memories to formulate her concept of good mothering. Kavita recalled her mother, a migrant to the UK, teaching the children at her school about elements of Indian culture, as Kavita has been doing at her daughter's daycare centre. Unlike her mother, Kavita has been able to draw on the online mothers' group for the knowledge, ideas, and confidence to support her in this: "I know that that can be done because my mum did that when I was in school, but it's a very different world that we live in now, and I might not have felt so confident about doing it if it wasn't for that group." Kavita also planned to teach cooking classes in her local area, "sending them home with spice packs, so they're getting confidence in spices." Through this work with her daughter's peers, and her own generation, Kavita hoped to engender "more integration of our culture into general society." Kavita's maternal projects can be understood through the lens of "community mothering" outlined in the previous chapter. Stretching beyond the mother–child dyad, Kavita advocates for a place for Indian culture – and by extension for her family – in her local, predominantly white, Australian community. Kavita deploys her imagined maternal community – imbued with childhood memories, a familial narrative of good motherhood, and liberal values of cultural diversity and acceptance – as a tool to change the Australian imagined national community.

For Stefanie and Kavita, embarking on motherhood after migration activated a sense of being part of imagined maternal communities, linked to their childhood, familial narratives, and national and ethnic identities. These attachments became salient to them in new ways as they moved into motherhood, and drove them to forge connections with mothers whom they understood to share this diasporic maternal identity. The local online diasporic mothers' groups provided a hub for these connections. As well as joining the Indian mothers' group, Kavita also joined the group for British and Irish mothers in her area and found comfort in being part of a community of mothers who shared her experience of raising her child a long way from family, missing British chocolate, and managing family visits, long flights, and migration-related guilt. Kavita's membership of the British and Irish group was less focused on her daughter's experience and more on her position as a British mother in Australia in relation to other British mothers in Australia. "Just knowing that they're there" and "hearing them pipe up about their stories and what's going on for them" enabled Kavita to construct a sense of a migrant maternal community from which she derives a sense of solidarity and "sisterhood": "just, you know, god, we're all in the same boat." Her memberships of the two groups positioned her within two imagined maternal communities, drew on different strands of her personal narrative, and enabled her to assemble the resources to meet her need for sociality and emotional support as a migrant woman with a disrupted social infrastructure, as well as her need for cultural connection and support in her project of "mothering for ethnicity" (Manohar 2013a). Motherhood drew Kavita and Stefanie into these imagined maternal communities, and they, in turn, drew their fellow migrant mothers closer to them in order to construct a sense of themselves as British-Indian, or German, mothers in Australia and to facilitate their maternal projects which would meet their standards of good motherhood.

Grounding imagined migrant maternal communities in shared values

Imagined maternal communities are structured according to different logics and underpinned by different values. Like many of the mothers' groups, the Swedish mothers' imagined maternal communities were grounded in a logic of shared experience, language, history, food, and practices. They were also grounded in what they understood to be a shared value of gender equality, which is underpinned by Swedish state legislation, policy, and rhetoric, such that "gender equality has been constructed as part of the [Swedish] national identity" (Kvist & Peterson 2010, p. 188). This was evident in the interviews with Swedish mothers. Jenni described Sweden as "culturally [...] gender equal," and throughout the interviews, gender equality emerged as a key theme, structuring their discussions of their decisions around gender roles, paid employment, their husbands' experiences around work and paternity leave, their aspirations for inculcating "Swedish values" in their children, and in the ways in which the groups formed and continued to operate.

Through their analysis of policy and political debates, Kvist and Peterson (2010) have demonstrated how the specific form of gender equality espoused in Sweden since the 1970s depended on state provision of childcare, elderly care, and other support services to increase men's involvement in caring and women's paid labour market participation.[1] The Swedish mothers in this study shared a sense that good Swedish motherhood involved dividing the responsibility and rewards of child-raising and paid employment equally between mothers and fathers and passing on a similar notion of gender equality to their children. While they still imagined themselves as part of a community of mothers who shared this value, this narrative was challenged by their lived experience of mothering away from the structural and social supports that underpinned it. Married to Australian and British men who did not share their identity-based commitment to gender equality, and living in Australia with its more limited state provision of childcare, less political commitment to gender equality, and more widespread acceptance of separate gender roles in parenting and work, they struggled to live up to their aspiration to mother in accordance with their Swedish values.

Lina described gender equality as "a Swedish value I would like my children to get," although she admitted that she and her husband had not modelled it in their division of domestic and paid labour. Besides their differing work patterns when the children were very young, Lina does "all the cooking" and "a lot more of the housework than he does, despite the fact that I'm working now." Lina described this arrangement as unsatisfactory, primarily because of the message it sends to their children: "We have to change that before they really grow up!" she laughed. However, she struggled to see how they could change it, in a context in which her husband's employers took little account of his parenting responsibilities:

> Even if he [husband] said, 'oh yeah, I can stay home,' in his profession a man is not really allowed to do that. Even though they say he is allowed, but it wouldn't be accepted that he hasn't produced anything. They can say as much as they want it's gender equality, it's not. It's not.

Here, Lina highlights the importance of unwritten rules based on gender ideology that can override official policies of gender neutrality. Eva had found it difficult to work in Australia because of her husband's inflexible employment and a lack of childcare beyond school hours. Apart from some periods of temporary, part-time employment as a nurse, Eva had mostly been at home with her son, who was three at the time of the interview, an arrangement she felt would have been unthinkable in Sweden. In terms of support for new mothers, Eva noted that her friends in Sweden provided less support to her as a new mother compared to the support offered by her friends in Australia when she arrived there with a three-month-old baby. Eva ascribed this to her Swedish friends' and family's expectation that new mothers' partners would be around to cook, whereas her friends in Australia provided meals for new mothers in their circle, knowing their spouses would not take on this role. Unfortunately for Eva, this meant that, alone in Sweden with her newborn baby after her husband returned to his job in Australia, she received very little hands-on support.

Eva, Lina, and Sabina drew on their lived experiences as mothers in Australia to explain their matricentric online groups, despite the apparent contradiction they presented to their commitment to gender equality in parenting. By contrast, Jenni drew on the values of her imagined community to explain the importance of including fathers in her online group:

> I don't want to bring my babies up in a world where it's like that. I want, I try to be very conscious about trying to be equal, trying to be … dads are just as much parents as mums.

Jenni articulates a personal narrative in which she, as a Swedish mother, has a vital role in educating her children in the Swedish value of gender equality. This personal narrative relates to a shared national narrative in which gender equality is an aspirational goal which takes conscious effort to achieve. Accordingly, Jenni's role extends further than her own children into the kind of "community mothering" discussed in an earlier chapter, in which she has a responsibility to shape the world around her, to reflect and encourage the enactment of that value. Jenni's investment in this "possible world" of gender equality (Kanno & Norton 2003, p. 248) influences how she frames her own parenting and how she runs her online group. For Lina, this "possible world" of gender equality exists in Sweden but not in Australia. This (im)possibility frames her judgement of her parenting and work practices as well as her hopes for her children. She pronounces herself "desperate to get them to become Swedish" and notes that while she speaks Swedish to her children "it's the whole values" she wishes to impart. Migration has challenged her understanding of herself as a Swedish mother who co-parents with her spouse to raise children with the same attachment to a value of gender equality. While Lina maintains a hopeful desire to re-balance her family and work life along more gender-neutral lines and provide an appropriate role model to her children, she acknowledges the structural constraints in an Australian context that inhibit that possibility. Migrant mothers who draw on imagined maternal communities and personal narratives grounded in values strongly underpinned by state and social institutions may find that the migrant context forces them to "renegotiate their identities as moral mothers" (Liamputtong 2006).

Materialising migrant maternal imaginaries in everyday practices and objects

We don't swaddle babies in Germany! You do not swaddle my baby!

(Katja)

Migrant mothers drew on their attachment to an imagined community of mothers to make and justify decisions about everyday maternal practices. In discussing the ways in which maternal practices in Germany differed from those they observed in Australia, German mothers mentioned a range of practices; for example, the widespread use of homeopathic products in Germany, the practice of giving tea to small babies, modes of bathing, state support for postnatal mothers, preferences around toys and games, parenting ethos, gendered child-raising, pedagogical approaches in childcare, use of 'natural' products, school starting age and school routines, breastfeeding, part-time working, and first foods for babies. Swaddling babies[2] was mentioned by most of the German, and some Swedish, mothers as a practice with which they had been unfamiliar prior to having a baby in Australia. This section focuses on the ways in which mothers navigated choices around swaddling.

Despite Annika's assertion that "I think you just step into it; you just do what other mums do here," all the German participants talked about the various ways they attempted to incorporate, or chose not to incorporate, elements of German maternal practice. For many of the German mothers, swaddling was a focal point for navigating their position as German mothers in Australia. While some adopted the practice, others resisted. Petra recalled: "That's where I lived my Germannness. We don't swaddle [laughs]. What the heck?!" Petra had moved to Australia three years before she became a mother for the first time. Nevertheless, she expressed strongly-held ideas about how maternal practices in Australia differed from those in Germany, and how these practices related to her sense of herself as a German mother. Katja, who had predominantly lived in Australia since leaving high school in Germany, remembered having arguments with the midwives in the hospital who tried to swaddle her baby. She told them: "We don't swaddle babies in Germany! You do not swaddle my baby!" By contrast, Heike chose to swaddle her babies but bathed them the way she knew from her upbringing in Germany:

> In Australia, we do swaddle them, so they don't wake themselves. I thought, this kind of works, and I did it with all three of them. […] So I swaddled my kids, but I stuck them in a bucket to bath them. […] Because the same reason for swaddling is the same reason Germans use for their bucket bath. Because it's like being in the womb and they like that confined space.

Heike positions herself as part of an Australian maternal community as well as a German one, drawing them together using a child-centred logic that positions infants as having instinctive preferences that transcend cultural differences. Many of the women in this study drew on a similar logic of efficacy to justify their decisions, adopting "whatever works" (Lina) and abandoning practices which "weren't working" (Aditi). In this context, what "worked" was often defined as what increased the amount of sleep achieved by the baby and therefore the mother. Resonating with the study of cross-national couples mentioned in this chapter's introduction (Adams 2004), women deploying the logic of efficacy attributed more validity to 'reality' and 'rationality' than to the maintenance of their position within an imagined maternal community. By contrast, Katja and Petra positioned themselves firmly within an imagined German maternal community, which does not swaddle its infants. It is noteworthy that the views of their Australian spouses on swaddling are conspicuously absent from their accounts.

All of the German mothers were apparently able to identify individual practices as "German" and others as "Australian." As first-time mothers in a new country, they brought with them knowledge and practices accumulated through their own upbringing and observations of maternal practices. These had accreted over time to form a narrative of themselves as German mothers, which lay largely unexamined until activated by their move into motherhood. Decision-making around maternal practices brought this narrative into focus, as it was challenged by alternative narratives and their lived experience of motherhood and baby care. These challenges to their maternal narrative could be confusing, as women struggled to decide which advice to follow, but it could also be liberating, giving them a critical distance to all proffered advice. They were also important moments of identity construction, as they enacted or shifted their attachments to their imagined communities, reconstructing or reconciling their personal narratives in their changed context.

In their discussions and decisions around everyday maternal practices, migrant mothers engaged with their maternal narratives as these narratives were challenged, ruptured, or re-shaped by the experience of migration. For some women, imagining themselves in relation to a national or ethnic maternal community produced a desire for everyday objects of motherhood, like toys, books, clothes, food, and remedies, and this desire drove them to participate in the online groups. German participants, in particular, spoke about procuring German toys and books for their children, relating them to a notion of German child-rearing, which they understood as more child-centred, more 'natural,' less technology-focused or competitive than the Australian practices they observed. Books represented both a practical means to share and impart mothers' language to their children and also a vehicle for particular values. Reflecting the centrality of "Swedish values" in her maternal practices, Jenni appreciated Swedish books for normalising diverse family formations and gender-equal parenting through the characters represented in the books, discussing "controversial things like death and spiritual stuff" and depicting a broader range of possibilities for childhood behaviour.

Objects also represent the nostalgic pull of home, or of their own childhood, a link to their individual journey to motherhood. Eva described how Swedish objects or brands enabled women "just to have a bit of Sweden with you." Jenni observed that Swedish parents in her group expressed a greater sense of trust in Swedish brands than in their Australian equivalents. Annika had recently bought twenty German children's story audio tapes from someone in an online group, despite not owning a working tape recorder. She drew on links with her childhood to explain her "excitement" about this purchase and suggested the tapes could provide a pathway to being a 'better' mother:

> My mum says we used to just listen to it all day and we'd have it with us all the time, and you know, it was our entertainment, there wasn't TV and now it's like iPads, phones, … And sometimes I feel bad, but I sometimes have no choice because I have to put my little one down and what does the older one do?

Annika implies that using older technologies like tapes to entertain children represents a morally superior parenting choice compared to contemporary technologies like "iPads, phones," reflecting popular discourses that position digital media as "risk amplifiers" that increase children's vulnerability and threaten normal development (Clark 2013, p. 6) or as "digital babysitters" used by "neglectful" parents (Steinkuehler 2016, p. 358). Annika positions herself within an imagined German maternal community that still makes use of such 'superior', older, technology, aligning herself with the German woman from whom she purchased the tapes as well as her own mother, for whom tapes were a memorable part of her mothering experience. Annika hopes her mother might bring a tape recorder from Germany when she next visits.

This chapter offers a broad argument about the migrant maternal imaginaries, and in line with the notion of motherhood as culturally and historically specific, which underpins this research, it is also important to examine some of the specific ways in which these imaginaries manifest. While mothers from all backgrounds discussed differences in everyday maternal practices, and linked these to an imagined sense of themselves as a mother from a particular place or community, this section has focused on some of the specific ways German migrant maternal imaginaries are materialised in maternal practices and objects. For German women, practices like swaddling, and objects like wooden toys and 'natural' products, were central to their migrant maternal imaginaries. By contrast, Indian women dwelt on practices like co-sleeping, care and rituals for pregnant and postnatal women, and expectations about collective care between family members. In the next section, I analyse the ways in which migrant mothers navigate alternative maternal imaginaries, drawing particularly on the experiences of Indian participants.

Navigating alternative migrant maternal imaginaries

In migration, women encounter unfamiliar beliefs about motherhood and maternal practices yet remain connected to the beliefs and practices of the community in which they were raised. Migration therefore requires women to navigate parallel beliefs about motherhood (DeSouza 2005) that are held by the imagined communities to which they perceive themselves as belonging. This can be difficult and stressful. However, the physical separation of migration can also offer some freedom from cultural constraints: mothers can leave behind the "interference" (Priya) and "over-involvement" (Kavita) of extended families or communities and "discard old ways of doing things" (DeSouza 2005, p. 91). Migration may offer access to an alternative imagined maternal community, one in which it is possible to mother differently. In this section, the focus is on how new mothers navigate family advice.

Some of the Indian mothers in this study contrasted a collective mode of motherhood – which they associated with an imagined Indian maternal community – with a more individualistic mode of motherhood, associated with an imagined Australian maternal community. Although the collective mode of motherhood offered the potential for increased social support and delegation of childcare and domestic tasks, individualised motherhood offered a sense of independence and self-determination which was also appealing. Priya imagined raising her children in India:

> It would have been very challenging for me to raise my child the way I want to raise. Because there is 17 people coming in every day telling you what to do, […] so it would have been difficult for me to say 'No, no, no, but this is what the research says. So, yes, you raised me this way, and I survived, but this is how I want to raise my child.' […] So, if I make my mistakes, they are my mistakes, it's my journey, and yes you support, but I'm still the one going through this journey.

Although Priya's mother, and then mother-in-law, lived with them in Melbourne for the first year of her baby's life, being situated in Australia enabled Priya to navigate a path between the professional advice she received from doctors and midwives, the research she read independently, and her personal experience of what "made sense" to her. Nisha articulated a similar view, positioning the imagined support she would receive in India as interfering with her maternal practices and as a hindrance to her mode of good motherhood:

> I know it takes a village to raise a child, but I think, like, even if there's a whole village, it's the mother that should have the biggest bond with them, the strongest bond with them, and that's just how it is for me.

During family visits, Nisha appreciated the help for a while but then reclaimed her maternal autonomy: "OK, you guys can stay here, but don't tell me what to do with my kids, no, [laughs], I can't cope with that." Nisha judged herself to be a better mother because she was more "hands-on" than the mothers she knew in India, who shared care with family and domestic staff. She felt she knew her children better and could better meet their needs. Her husband worked long hours away from home and was unable to participate fully in child raising, but Nisha claimed, "I would rather do it my way."

Aditi strategically deployed her position as a migrant mother to validate her choices of maternal practice. When her mother offered unwelcome advice about when to bathe her baby, Aditi used her mother's absence to rebuff her advice: "I'm here by myself, I need to do what works, and if you want to give me your advice, you better move here and help me out, and then I'll do it your way." At other times, Aditi used her mother's support for co-sleeping and "feeding to sleep" to validate her decision to dismiss dominant Australian advice to avoid those practices:

> Mum was OK about feeding to sleep, whereas here we recommend don't feed to sleep. [...] So I was told here: don't fall asleep with your baby. My mother slept with me when I was a baby [...] in the same bed. I was fine. I slept with my son in the same bed. And they said then the transition to cot will be difficult. It wasn't.

Like Heike in the previous section, Aditi positions herself as part of both an Australian maternal community – "here we recommend don't feed to sleep" – and an imagined maternal community linked to her country and family of origin, and her own experience of being mothered. Awareness of alternative frameworks and beliefs enables migrant mothers to approach dominant practices with a degree of scepticism and distance that leaves more room for personal choice than their non-migrant counterparts might experience. As a new mother in Singapore, Aoife drew on her personal network of "physio friends" in the UK and Ireland to help her decide whether to pursue a treatment for her baby. Her refusal "horrified" her practitioner in Singapore, and Aoife felt she had been judged "a delinquent parent" as a result. Nevertheless, her ability to draw on alternative expertise and frameworks of "good parenting" enabled Aoife to shrug off this judgement and relate it as a humorous encounter. In Heike's words, "I actually picked what suited me, and I still sort of do that. [...] Because I have access to two different cultures of raising kids." Lina felt her experience, becoming a mother in China as a Swedish temporary migrant before moving to Australia, gave her the freedom to choose her own path. Away from their mothers ("mums have a lot of ideas about things," she laughed) and already planning their move away from China, Lina felt she didn't "have to listen" to anyone. Instead, she described relying on her "own reasoning" and "logic." Lina compared this to her peers in Australia, who "felt horrible" if they were not able to breastfeed, due to the perceived pressure from health professionals to breastfeed.

Alongside the migrant-specific maternal online groups, many of the women had also joined local online mothers' groups aimed at all mothers in the local area. These generic mothers' groups offered rapid insights into local maternal norms and practices. Jenni reflected on the ways her maternal practices had been influenced by her observation of these generic local mothers' online groups. For example, she insisted her parents get vaccinated against whooping cough when they came to visit her newborn baby, having observed local mothers discussing it on the online groups of which she was a member:

> Looking back on it now, I didn't even reflect about that; maybe it was a bit extreme. [...] Other people did that, so I thought... oh you know... which maybe was a bit extreme. [...] I wouldn't do that today.

Generic local online mothers' groups were a means by which women became aware of local maternal norms and practices alongside information gleaned from Australian pregnancy manuals and baby books, and interactions with health professionals. They were also a means by which women imagined themselves as part of a local community of mothers in Australia.

Navigating between practices that resonated with an imagined national or ethnic maternal community and those which positioned them within a local community of mothers in Australia did not always bring relief or freedom. For some women, the negotiations were more fraught. Maria described placating her mother by telling her she had adhered to a Colombian practice, even when she had not. The disapproving reaction of her mother and mother-in-law to the news that Maria was not sleeping in the same room as the baby left her feeling "so guilty, so, so guilty." The decision to move the baby to a separate room had been the result of tense negotiations with Maria's husband, based on their need for sleep and space for themselves as a couple, but was unthinkable to their own mothers. Maria's parents-in-law stayed with them for six weeks after the baby's birth. Despite the practical support they provided – "for six weeks, we didn't look after the house, didn't do anything at home, didn't cook a thing, we didn't go to the supermarket" – Maria remembered her anger at the unsolicited advice offered by her mother-in-law, which conflicted with what she had chosen to do:

There were moments that it was like 'arrgghhh! Just let me do whatever I want to do!' And now I know she didn't do it because she wants me to do it her way, she was just probably giving an opinion, but in that moment, it sounded like she was telling me 'you are doing something wrong.'

As women remained connected to imagined maternal communities linked to their national or ethnic identities, they also forged connections with imagined maternal communities in their new location. These new connections challenged the continuity of the maternal narratives women carried with them. Women responded to those challenges in different ways. At times, Maria drew on a sense of connection to Colombian motherhood to justify practices which differed from the Australian norm: "When I was with my [Australian] mothers' group, I wouldn't do it, but when I was at home I would do it because I would think it was the right thing to do, or everybody does it in Colombia." At other times, Maria used the rupture in her maternal narrative to assert a sense of self-determination: "The things I didn't believe, I didn't do it." As illustrated above, asserting a disconnection to her maternal community, represented by her mother and mother-in-law, had emotional consequences including guilt, fear of judgement, and anger in response to familial disapproval. Migrant mothers actively create new modes of mothering that draw on culturally based maternal narratives, and they respond to changing circumstances and challenges to those narratives. Nevertheless, migration is not a guaranteed pathway to self-determination. In the next section, I focus on two Indian participants' experiences with infertility to analyse the ways in which migration may offer freedom in the form of release from stigma, but at the same time that stigma may be maintained within migrant communities.

Navigating maternal taboos in migration: Infertility

Migration and the resulting shifting attachments to imagined maternal communities were particularly significant in navigating issues of stigma and taboo. In an Indian context, in which motherhood is often viewed as the ultimate, compulsory, and sacred destiny for all women (Manohar & Busse-Cárdenas 2011), infertility is often highly stigmatised (Riessman 2000). Pooja and Jyoti, both of whom had migrated from India to marry fiancés already living in Australia, explained how their experiences with infertility related to migration. Pooja, a 37-year-old senior manager who had migrated to Australia four years before our interview, contrasted the taboo surrounding infertility in India with the openness and lack of judgement with which friends and colleagues in Australia discussed IVF:

What helped me was I had so many women in my office who had gone through IVF and so on, and they were very open about it. So, at some point I started thinking, well, maybe that's what I need to do. You know, because there's other people that have gone through it and they're happy to share that experience, you don't feel like it's something horrible, like you feel it's alright. But in India that wouldn't be the case. Definitely not when I was there; maybe things have changed now, but definitely not when I was there.

Migration brought new people and perspectives into her immediate maternal community, enabling her to receive treatment for her gynaecological health issues. Distance from her friends and extended family enabled her to avoid the judgemental surveillance she would have experienced in India.

Like Pooja, Jyoti migrated to Sydney to marry her fiancé, but it had taken them twelve years to conceive their daughter. While Pooja expressed a sense that migration had liberated her from the stigma surrounding infertility, Jyoti described how the same stigma persisted in her network of Indian friends in Sydney. The intrusive questioning and pity she received from their Indian social circle led her to distance herself from them, preferring the company of "Australians, or other communities," who respected her privacy in this matter:

When we moved, of course we made a couple of Indian friends. And all of them were couples like us, and in the course, they all fell pregnant, had kids, one after another. So you become a childless couple, with a group of families that have got kids […] and sometimes you could see the pity in their eyes for you.

Jyoti's experience is a reminder that migrant communities, while a potential source of support for each other, can also act as a mechanism for surveillance and judgement, particularly of women's behaviour (Manohar 2013b, p. 49). Jyoti's response to her community's judgement was to distance herself, and that continued into motherhood. While she remained a member of the Indian mothers' group, she maintained a critical distance from it, asserting that she "thinks differently" to other members. By contrast, she was an enthusiastic participant in her local (non-migrant-specific) online mothers' group, finding it a valuable source of support for raising her daughter. She referred to it as her main source of "counsel" and connection to other mothers in her area. Jyoti used the Indian mothers' group to find information and services, and she participated in discussions. But she maintained that she derived little sense of emotional attachment or belonging from the Indian group, attributing this to their "different mindset" and her belief that they disagree on some fundamental issues. While Pooja felt liberated from the stigma of infertility after migration, for Jyoti that stigma persisted in her post-migration co-ethnic networks, leading her to seek sociality and emotional support elsewhere. Nevertheless, it was her migration to Sydney that provided Jyoti with alternative maternal networks in which she could navigate maternity and infertility without fear of stigma.

The role of memory in constructing imagined maternal communities and narratives

Women's memories of childhood, of being mothered, and of witnessing mothering connect them to their imagined maternal communities. Those individual memories are also layered with cultural memories and family narratives, creating strong attachments to a "maternal commons" that endures across time and borders (Baraitser 2012). As discussed above, women carry this "culture of bonds" (Diminescu 2008) with them as they move countries, with it sometimes remaining latent until activated by impending motherhood. Women also forge new connections in migration, creating attachments with new imagined maternal communities which may offer new possibilities, conflict, or distress. In their interviews, some women drew on childhood memories, emphasising the importance of memory to their mothering. Situating themselves in an individual maternal narrative that stretched from their own childhood into a future represented by their children, women centred themselves in the middle of an idealised unbroken narrative in which part of their maternal role was to replicate parts of their own childhood experiences in their mothering practices. Migration had made that impossible, fracturing the continuity of their individual maternal narrative, leading to a sense of loss and sadness. This suggests that as well as having a past, women's maternal narratives also have an imagined future, which may be disrupted by migration. Unable to deploy memories in their present mothering and therefore unable to share them with their children, women expressed a sense of loss and discontinuity, as those memories must remain only in the past.

Michelle recalled memories of her English childhood "digging up worms" while exploring her local forest, explaining that she wanted the same experiences for her son, but this had been jeopardised by moving to a country containing dangerous Australian spiders and plants:

> My god, is my son ever actually going to go and play in the garden? And it's like what I'm kind of brought up with, and I kind of hoped he would go and lift rocks and stuff, and because I wasn't born here, and I don't know what the dangers are, and I don't know what's safe and what isn't..."

As she describes herself in this narrative, Michelle appears to be at risk of failing to perform two of Sara Ruddick's three key maternal practices: preserving her child's life and fostering his "physical, emotional, and intellectual growth" (Ruddick 1980, p. 348). Or rather, she fears that her attempts to preserve his life – by restricting his garden exploration – might hinder his growth. Migration has caused an epistemic deficit that jeopardises Michelle's attempts to draw on her childhood memories to frame her notions of what good motherhood involves. The practices of her imagined maternal community have less salience in her family's new environment.

Some women expressed a deep sense of nostalgic longing for their childhood, and a sense of loss at their inability to curate their children's experiences to include the same memories. Rebecca described "struggling" with the fact that her six-year-old daughter would not experience elements of her own childhood in south-east England, such as "easy travel to Europe" and "playing in the parks that I used to." Rebecca's wistful childhood memories of the "excitement of waking up to snow, big family lunches [...and...] the contrast of the seasons" were echoed in Susie's nostalgic recollections of sheltering from inclement British weather with "decent TV," board games and "a nice roast dinner on a Sunday," experiences she desired for her own children. Sheila conjured up vivid images from her Malaysian childhood of being "dragged into the kitchen" with her cousins to help cook for festivals; "being privy to adult gossip" during extended family gatherings; playing in the street with neighbours' children; and speaking multiple languages and dialects with her extended family. As much as she tried to replicate elements of her childhood, she noted regretfully, "it's still not the experience like we had as children, being taken by an uncle to go fish in an abandoned tin mine. You know, go swim in the rivers, and just to experience all of that. We just don't have it here." In acknowledging the impossibility of replicating those experiences, the women recognise the ruptures to their personal and family narratives resulting from migration, and the sadness that engenders for them.

Memories of childhood experiences were attached to notions of home and national identity for many women. The inability to share childhood experiences of home with their children introduces a discontinuity in their personal narrative that runs from 'being mothered' to 'mothering' and troubles their attempts to instil a sense of national or ethnic identity which would link their children (future) to their own childhood (past). Lina recognised that her childhood was a form of 'home' temporally as well as geographically inaccessible to her children: "my home is my childhood home that doesn't really exist, but that's in my mind." Home for Lina is the Swedish landscape and language, Swedish values and identity. While she can teach them to speak Swedish, the "greenness, and the lakes and the trees in Sweden" encapsulate a sense of home that she cannot share with her two children, who relate more to "eucalyptus and wallabies." While the Swedish landscape may remain relatively unchanged and accessible at least by visits home, Lina expressed a sense that the values she identifies as Swedish belong only in the past: "the values of my childhood is not the same any more in Sweden, so I don't know. My idea of Swedish might not be actual Swedish." Susie has tried hard to instil a sense of 'Britishness' in her Australian-born children, drawing on childhood memories to formulate the skills and experiences that a good British mother helps her children to attain, such as resilience to bad weather and boredom, and a "quirky sense of humour." Susie's sense of failure is palpable when she describes how her youngest child "waves an Australian flag around the house, singing the national anthem." She sighs, "it's really weird, and it's not what I wanted. But then I've created it." Susie appears to be articulating a responsibility to teach her children how to cope with everyday conditions to which they are no longer exposed: inclement British weather, and the resulting indoor lifestyle. She is frustrated by her failure to perform this element of maternal practice, which may be just a residual shadow of a no longer relevant maternal project.

This sense of failure resonated with some of the other mothers. Usha expressed this explicitly:

> It's very nice that he adapts, he's able to adapt himself, you know, adapt to different countries, and adapt himself for different cultures. But for me, I feel somewhere have I failed as a parent, to not instil in him what India really means to him.

The impossibility of replicating their own childhood experiences, and transmitting the skills, values, and emotional significance embedded in those memories, highlighted the rupture in their maternal narratives. They worried that this discontinuity might create emotional distance between them and their children. Aditi noted, "some things that mean so much to me, they mean nothing to them. And that's kind of disappointing." Nicole, perturbed by her 18-year-old Australian-raised daughter's values, communication style, and outlook, planned to return to Europe so her two younger children could grow up with a more similar outlook and experience to her own. These experiences suggest that "mothering for ethnicity" is not just about preserving culture as a common good that can be passed down the generations. It is also about nurturing bonds between mother and child and maintaining a sense of continuity in women's maternal narratives into an imagined future. While some elements of maternal narratives can be productively re-worked or reconciled in migration, the way women spoke about childhood memories, home, and identity suggests that some elements may be irrecoverably lost, causing a melancholic sense of maternal failure.

Conclusion

Migrant mothers, even first-time mothers, bring with them knowledge, practice, and values accumulated through their upbringing and observations of maternal practices. These accretions of knowledge, practice, and values form a narrative of themselves as mothers in relation to an imagined national community, which often lies largely unexamined until activated by their move into motherhood. Decision-making around maternal practices brought this narrative into focus, as it was challenged by alternative narratives and their lived experience of motherhood and baby care. These challenges to their maternal narrative could be confusing, as women struggled to decide which advice to follow, but they could also be liberating, giving them a critical distance to all proffered advice. They were also important moments of identity construction, as they enacted or shifted their attachments to their imagined communities, reconstructing or reconciling their personal narratives in their changed context. Nevertheless, some elements of their maternal narratives were not able to be reconstructed or reconciled after the rupture of migration. The irrecoverable loss of these elements, encapsulated in the childhood memories discussed above, produced a sense of sadness and maternal failure, which some women struggled to overcome.

The role of the digital in managing the ruptures and connections of migrant motherhood is multi-faceted. Digital connections in the form of localised migrant maternal online communities provided opportunities for migrant mothers to discuss their decision-making around maternal practices, their observations of local maternal practices, and their attempts to incorporate or resist culturally inflected elements into their mothering. Membership of these groups can be seen as a way of positioning themselves within particular imagined maternal communities. Joining online groups aimed at local mothers generally (not just migrant mothers) enabled migrant women to observe local maternal norms and practices, and offered the possibility of aligning themselves with an Australian maternal community. Other forms of digital connection challenged or confirmed women's shifting attachments. For example, online connections with family and friends back home facilitated surveillance and judgement of those practices at a distance. When Jenni and Eva adopted the locally dominant practice of swaddling, photographs posted online provided the opportunity for family members to comment or criticise. Eva recalled: "they thought I was trapping him, like he couldn't move!"

At particular moments in their migrant mothering, some women make sense of their choices and emotions through the lens of an ethnic or national imaginary, which can be seen to inhere in the online groups. In a more abstract sense, the groups function metonymically, standing in for a wider imagined community. The existence of the group confirms that other people 'like them' exist, even if they are not all members of the specific online group. The group represents 'the image of their communion' (Anderson 2006 [1983], p. 6), a representation of their collective maternal imaginary, as well as a mechanism for forging 'real' connections with other members of the community. The groups become attractive, or relevant, as their maternal narrative becomes activated in the journey to motherhood or migration. Discussions facilitated by the group help women to respond to challenges to their maternal narrative, help them re-shape their narrative and reconcile their hopes and desires with their lived experience, or to comfort each other in their shared experiences of loss.

Notes

1 Relevant to the intersections of migration and motherhood, Kvist and Peterson (2010) outline how the retraction of the welfare state in the 1990s left a gap which was increasingly filled by migrant domestic workers to safeguard (non-migrant, middle-class) women's participation in the workplace. Men's participation in the workplace was not seen to be jeopardised by the withdrawal of state provision of childcare.
2 Firm wrapping of a baby in a piece of material for the purposes of "settling an infant and promoting supine sleep positioning" (Young et al. 2013).

References

Adams, J. (2004). The imagination and social life. *Qualitative Sociology*, 27(3), 277–297. doi:10.1023/B:QUAS.0000037619.28845.ef.

Anderson, B. R. O. G. (2006). *Imagined communities: Reflections on the origin and spread of nationalism*. New York; London: Verso (Original work published 1983).

Baraitser, L. (2012). Communality across time: Responding to encounters with maternal encounters: The ethics of interruption. *Studies in Gender and Sexuality*, 13(2), 117–122. doi:10.1080/15240657.2012.682932.

Clark, L. S. (2013). *The parent app: Understanding families in the digital age*. New York; Oxford:Oxford University Press.

Collins, P. H. (2000). Black women and motherhood. In *Black feminist thought* (pp. 173–199). Revised 10th anniversary ed. Routledge.

DeSouza, R. (2005). Transforming possibilities of care: Goan migrant motherhood in New Zealand. *Contemporary Nurse: A Journal for the Australian Nursing Profession*, 20, 87–101. doi:10.5172/conu.20.1.87.

Diminescu, D. (2008). The connected migrant: An epistemological manifesto. *Social Science Information*, 47(4), 565–579.

Gedalof, I. (2009). Birth, belonging and migrant mothers: Narratives of reproduction in feminist migration studies. *Feminist Review*, 93(1), 81–100.

Goodwin, S., & Huppatz, K. (2010). *The good mother: Contemporary motherhoods in Australia*. Sydney, NSW: Sydney University Press.

Ho, C. (2006). Migration as feminisation? Chinese women's experiences of work and family in Australia. *Journal of Ethnic and Migration Studies*, 32(3), 497–514.

Hondagneu-Sotelo, P., & Avila, E. (1997). "I'm here but I'm there": The meanings of Latina transnational motherhood. *Gender & Society*, 11(5), 548–571. doi:10.1177/089124397011005003.

Kanno, Y., & Norton, B. (2003). Imagined communities and educational possibilities: Introduction. *Journal of Language, Identity & Education*, 2(4), 241–249. doi:10.1207/S15327701JLIE0204_1.

Keller, J. (2010). Rethinking Ruddick and the ethnocentrism critique of "maternal thinking". *Hypatia*, 25(4), 834–851. doi:10.1111/j.1527-2001.2010.01139.x.

Kvist, E., & Peterson, E. (2010). What has gender equality got to do with it? An analysis of policy debates surrounding domestic services in the welfare states of Spain and Sweden. *NORA - Nordic Journal of Feminist and Gender Research*, 18(3), 185–203. doi:10.1080/08038740.2010.498326.

Liamputtong, P. (2006). Motherhood and "moral career": Discourses of good motherhood among Southeast Asian immigrant women in Australia. *Qualitative Sociology*, 29(1), 25–53. doi:10.1007/s11133-005-9006-5.

Madianou, M. (2012). Migration and the accentuated ambivalence of motherhood: The role of ICTs in Filipino transnational families. *Global Networks*, 12(3), 277–295. doi:10.1111/j.1471-0374.2012.00352.x.

Manohar, N. N. (2013a). Mothering for class and ethnicity: The case of Indian professional immigrants in the United States. *Advances in Gender Research*, 17, 159–185. doi:10.1108/S1529-2126(2013)0000017011.

Manohar, N. N. (2013b). Support networks, ethnic spaces, and fictive kin: Indian immigrant women constructing community in the United States. *AAPI Nexus: Policy, Practice and Community*, 11(1–2), 25–55. doi:10.17953/appc.11.1-2.t81xj18224638u44.

Manohar, N. N., & Busse-Cárdenas, E. (2011). Valuing "good" motherhood in migration: The experiences of Indian professional wives in America and Peruvian working-class wives left behind in Peru. *Journal of the Motherhood Initiative for Research and Community Involvement*, 2(2), 175–195.

Meyers, C., & Rugunanan, P. (2020). Mobile-mediated mothering from a distance: A case study of Somali mothers in Port Elizabeth, South Africa. *International Journal of Cultural Studies*, 23(5), 656–673. doi:10.1177/1367877920926645.

Riessman, C. K. (2000). Stigma and everyday resistance practices: Childless women in South India. *Gender and Society*, 14(1), 111–135.

Ruddick, S. (1980). Maternal thinking. *Feminist Studies*, 6(2), 342–367. doi:10.2307/3177749.

Steinkuehler, C. (2016). Parenting and video games. *Journal of Adolescent & Adult Literacy*, 59(4), 357–361. doi:10.1002/jaal.455.

Thurer, S. (1995). *The myths of motherhood: How culture reinvents the good mother.* New York: Penguin (Original work published 1994).

Utomo, A. (2014). Mother tongue, mothering, and (transnational) identity: Indonesian mothers in Canberra, Australia. *ASEAS - Austrian Journal of South-East Asian Studies*, 7(2), 165–182. doi:10.14764/10.ASEAS-2014.2-3.

Young, J., Gore, R., Gorman, B., & Watson, K. (2013). Wrapping and swaddling infants: Child health nurses' knowledge, attitudes and practice. *Neonatal, Paediatric & Child Health Nursing*, 16(3), 2–11.

Ziaian, T. (2000). The psychological effects of migration on Persian women immigrants in Australia. (Doctoral dissertation). Retrieved from https://digital.library.adelaide.edu.au/dspace/handle/2440/19666.

6   Concluding reflections

Introduction

> If there was ever a time where I did feel that I was away from my community, was when I had my son, because [...] I have built myself a life here, but my life here was very much around being single or partnered. I didn't have [...] a day life; I didn't know what happened in our neighbourhood during the day, because I had never had a life when I was home during the day. I didn't know anybody who was home during the day. And it was almost like I moved to a new country, because I had to re-do the whole integration thing. You know, find new people, find a whole new community.
>
> (Sabina, creator of Scandinavian mothers' group)

This book set out to examine the experiences of contemporary migrant mothers in Australia through the lens of migrant maternal online communities. Through analysis of data generated by scoping, survey, and semi-structured interview methods, those online communities have been shown to function on instrumental, relational, affective, and metonymic levels. As Sabina indicates in her comments quoted above, both migration and motherhood require women to find a "new community," and this book has explored the new communities that migrant mothers build for themselves online. In a context in which theorising about motherhood has drawn only lightly on migrant mothers' experiences, and theorising about migration has sidelined experiences of mothers, this book has centred the experiences of migrant mothers. A feminist-inflected focus on the "micropolitics of everyday life" (Mohanty 2003, p. 509), combined with a matricentric feminist emphasis on maternal practices, has brought to the surface some key findings about the everyday lives of migrant mothers in Australia. Specifically, it has drawn attention to their intentional, relational, digital, and community practices, positioning each of these as work. These findings encompass the practical, emotional, and imaginative consequences of migration, motherhood, and the combination of both. For example, the gendered nature of parenting in Australia is made clear in the practices within the online groups and the participants' rationalisation of those practices, drawing on everyday experiences and gendered discourses around sociality, responsibility, support needs, and parenting.

Intersectionality has framed this book's findings with its attention to multiple axes of difference and to the relationality that emphasises the interconnectedness of people and the centrality of the network of relationships of which we are a part. Rather than proceeding from an understanding of migrant maternal identities as essentialised, atomised spaces of difference (which stand in comparison to each other and to a White Australian 'norm'), this research has explored how those self-understandings are constructed and materialised, how they interconnect, and how they differ. The findings point to the importance of the imagination for the construction and manifestation of intersectional identities. For these migrant mothers, motherhood is something that is imagined, remembered, and desired, as well as practised and negotiated in relation to their families, communities, and culturally based narratives, and, crucially, in relation to other mothers.

Summary of findings

An analysis of the digital and emotional labour performed by the groups' administrators (conceptualised here as *meta-maternal practices*) has laid bare how migrant mothers play a vital role in supporting each other's settlement in Australia. These practices, which include boundary work, emotional curation, and social facilitation, create spaces for migrant mothers online, which are characterised by trust, similarity, and sociality. I have argued that this role constitutes *digital community mothering*, a kind of community service performed mostly but not entirely online, in which women take on responsibility for the wellbeing of children, mothers, and families in their community. This community service may be experienced as exhausting, but it also brings pride and satisfaction. The administrators' digital nurturing of their communities and the mothers who constitute those communities encourages a mode of *compassionate mothering* between group members, which helps mothers to transcend differences in maternal practice and to build migrant maternal solidarities.

Over time, some of these accidental community managers have become *accidental community leaders*. The visibility of their leadership within their migrant maternal online communities spills out into the public spaces of their local community, into their workplaces and their partners' workplaces, bringing pride and social status but also vulnerability. This visibility and leadership – forged in these communities which transcend domestic space – trouble a binary social imaginary that associates motherhood with privacy, domesticity, and intimate care. This book has also made migrant mothers' digital community labour and leadership visible in the context of academic scholarship. By positioning mothers as both consumers and producers of digital information and community, and as active agents working to effect settlement and create belonging for themselves and others, this book works to bring mothers out from the shadows of migration and digital social research.

The administrators' creation and curation of the online groups enable other migrant mothers to fulfil their gendered settlement responsibilities to their family, to effect their own relational and affective settlement, and to position themselves within a migrant maternal imaginary. Mothers use the affordances of the groups to create and access forms of intimacy, support, and belonging that are necessary to their wellbeing, and which their existing networks of family and friends cannot provide. In the groups, they are able to rebuild their social infrastructure, which has been disrupted by migration and motherhood, and co-construct with each other a sense of companionship, reassurance, comfort, and belonging.

By exchanging information and forging social connections, migrant mothers help each other to build a new home for their family after the disruption of migration. Furthermore, they support women to meet their own needs for friendship and social interaction. Social connections at all levels, from casual intimacy to heartfelt friendship, are fundamental to building a new locally emplaced sense of belonging. The groups are spaces where mothers can generate new senses of belonging based on shared migrant maternal experiences. In this book, I have called this process of building belonging through social connections *relational settlement*. Through these social connections, migrant mothers become an affective resource for each other, helping each other to manage their complex emotional responses to migration and motherhood and, in some cases, to reconcile ongoing negative emotions with the possibility of belonging. This collective and individual emotion work – which has the aim of generating a sense of belonging and comfort out of disruption and discomfort – I have called *affective settlement*.

Diving deeper into this idea of settlement through affective practices, this book has examined the role of the digital in managing the ruptures and connections of migrant motherhood. Digital connections in the form of localised migrant maternal online communities provide opportunities for migrant mothers to discuss their decision-making around maternal practices, their observations of local maternal practices, and their attempts to incorporate or resist culturally inflected elements into their mothering. Discussions facilitated by the groups help women respond to the challenges to their maternal narrative, help them re-shape their narrative and reconcile their hopes and desires with their lived experience, or provide comfort in their shared experiences of loss.

The book has presented the concepts of migrant maternal narratives and migrant maternal imagined communities. A *migrant maternal narrative* is a personal narrative of oneself as a mother in relation to an imagined national community, and which often lies largely unexamined until activated by matrescence, the move into motherhood (Raphael 1975). Those narratives are formed from an accretion of knowledge, practice, and values accumulated through their upbringing and observations of maternal practices. Drawing on the rich experiences of the women I interviewed, this book has shown how these maternal narratives are challenged by the alternative narratives encountered after migration, and by their lived experiences of motherhood and raising children in a migrant context. In response to these challenges, migrant mothers enact or shift their attachments to their imagined communities, reconstructing or reconciling their personal narratives in their changed context. Some women found elements of their maternal narratives that were not able to be reconstructed or reconciled, and this produced a sense of loss, sadness, and maternal failure.

Mothers position themselves within particular *imagined maternal communities*, and one way they do this is by creating or joining online groups that reflect their community attachment. Joining a group is, in part, a performative act of attachment to a migrant maternal identity. The groups are sites in which women's attachments to their diasporic maternal community are forged and re-confirmed. They also act as a material form of community, a means by which fellow migrant mothers become visible to each other, interact with each other, and form relationships. The existence of the group confirms that other people 'like them' exist, even if they are not all members of the specific online group. It is a representation of their *collective maternal imaginary* as well as a mechanism for forging 'real' connections with other members of the community. Maternal identities, migrant identities, and migrant maternal identities are not singular or mutually exclusive. The heterogeneity of the social media landscape affords people the opportunity to join multiple groups, to perform numerous and nuanced acts of attachment to more than one community or identity, and to tailor their online experience to meet their personal and mutable needs.

Significance and future focus

In the preceding section, I have summarised the key findings from this research project. In this section, I highlight some of the significance of these findings and sketch in broad outline some of the concrete ways in which what has been learnt could be applied to improve the support offered to migrant mothers and their families. The importance of *connections between mothers* – both tangible and imagined – and *the role of the imaginary* in mothers' shifting and complex intersectional identities provides important insights into the ways in which mothers respond to the ongoing challenges of motherhood. It suggests that encouraging and facilitating these lateral relationships between mothers is important not just to manage the 'transition to motherhood,' as has been widely argued, but also to support ongoing maternal wellbeing. A recent review of research on migrant families' transnational ties and the implications for health and social care around pregnancy, birth, and early childhood (Merry et al. 2020) found "little evidence [...] that transnational ties, in terms of 'ways of being' [practices and relations], are acknowledged and addressed by care providers" (p. 19). The concept of *imagined communities of maternal practice*, in association with which mothers construct, reconstruct and reconcile their personal maternal narratives, is a significant contribution to the literature on motherhood and migration. For those working to support mothers in Australia's diverse communities, the concepts of *imagined maternal communities* and *maternal narratives* could be used to deepen understanding of mothers' attachments and resistances to specific maternal practices, which could inform the design and implementation of maternal support services.

Following on from that suggestion, this book also provides important insights into the kinds of information, emotional support, and social support that migrant mothers need. In the literature around migrant motherhood, particularly around post-partum mental health and isolation, there is a tendency for studies to end with a call for more "social support" for migrant mothers, without defining either the parameters of that social support or how it might be brought into existence. While this study was not designed to specifically answer those questions, by exploring the networks and activities instigated by migrant mothers themselves we can gain a clearer idea of their needs. Given the current enthusiasm for online interventions in maternal health (see, for example, AlJaberi 2018; George et al. 2012; Jones et al. 2013; Kernot et al. 2013), an exploration of what migrant mothers design for themselves, using the easily accessible affordances of Facebook, could provide a useful starting point for new interventions. At the very least, health and social care practitioners might find it useful to signpost these kinds of Facebook groups to their migrant mother clients.

Researchers and policymakers interested in increasing social cohesion and successful settlement after migration may find useful the findings that online communities can facilitate both locally emplaced senses of belonging and belonging relating to more geographically and temporally distant attachments, and can assist migrants in navigating and negotiating between these shifting and multiple attachments of belonging. While not dismissing the concerns that digital technologies can be used to create "virtual ghettos" (Komito & Bates 2012, p. 107) or "echo chambers" (Del Vicario et al. 2016), this research has found that migrant mothers use online communities tailored to their needs, alongside other tailored and generic, online and offline, sources of information and support to make a place for themselves in their local community and build new attachments to their local community.

Organisations supporting the settlement of migrants in Australia might consider encouraging migrants to join, participate in, or create similar online communities. Support organisations might consider providing resources, guidelines, and training to facilitate the participation of migrants who might not have used or created such online communities before. Tailored training for potential administrators addressing both technical issues and advice on successful facilitation could improve the support offered in migrant-specific online communities. Community organisations could approach the administrators of existing online communities and propose joint social events or seminars, co-production of information resources, and other partnership activities. Grant-making institutions might encourage such activities to increase the impact and reach of their funding programmes and to ensure the voluntary labour of group administrators is appropriately recognised.

In closing the book, I would like to return to the voices of the migrant mothers whose stories form the heart of the research. I hope I have done justice to their experiences.

I have also learned that I am not the only one going through some sort of stress, that there are other people in the same boat, so if I want I can reach out and there will be two people holding my hand. Having that support is really, really important. And it just makes me feel so much more grounded and secure wherever I am.

(Nisha, creator of the South Asian mothers' group)

References

AlJaberi, H. (2018). Social interaction needs and entertainment approaches to pregnancy well-being in health technology design for low-income transmigrant women: Qualitative codesign study. *JMIR – Journal of Medical Internet Research*, 6(4), e61. doi:10.2196/mhealth.7708.

Del Vicario, M., Vivaldo, G., Bessi, A., Zollo, F., Scala, A., Caldarelli, G., & Quattrociocchi, W. (2016). Echo chambers: Emotional contagion and group polarization on Facebook. *Scientific Reports*, 6, 37825. doi:10.1038/srep37825.

George, A., Duff, M., Ajwani, S., Johnson, M., Dahlen, H., Blinkhorn, A., Ellis, S., Bhole, S. (2012). Development of an online education program for midwives in Australia to improve perinatal oral health. *The Journal of Perinatal Education*, 21(2), 112–122. doi:10.1891/1058-1243.21.2.112.

Jones, B. A., Griffiths, K. M., Christensen, H., Ellwood, D., Bennett, K., & Bennett, A. (2013). Online cognitive behaviour training for the prevention of postnatal depression in at-risk mothers: A randomised controlled trial protocol. *BMC Psychiatry*, 13(1), 265. doi:10.1186/1471-244X-13-265.

Kernot, J., Olds, T., Lewis, L. K., & Maher, C. (2013). Effectiveness of a Facebook-delivered physical activity intervention for post-partum women: A randomized controlled trial protocol. *BMC Public Health*, 13 (1), 518. doi:10.1186/1471-2458-13-518.

Komito, L., & Bates, J. (2012). Migration, community and social media. In G. Boucher, A. Grindsted, & T. L. Vicente (Eds.), *Transnationalism in the global city* (pp. 97–112). Bilbao, Spain: Universidad de Deusto.

Merry, L., Fredsted Villadsen, S., Sicard, V., & Lewis-Hibbert, N. (2020). Transnationalism and care of migrant families during pregnancy, postpartum and early-childhood: An integrative review. *BMC Health Services Research*, 20(1), 1–24. doi:10.1186/s12913-020-05632-5.

Mohanty, C. T. (2003). *Feminism without borders: Decolonizing theory, practicing solidarity*. New Delhi: Zubaan.

Raphael, D. (1975). Matrescence, becoming a mother, a new / old rite de passage. In *Being female: Reproduction, power, and change*. Berkeley: University of California.

Appendix 1

The participants

Table A.1 Overview of the migrant maternal online communities included in the research

Place of origin	Place of residence[1]	No. of members (at time of administrator interview)	Administrators interviewed	Members interviewed	Year of group creation	Intentionally women-only?[2]
UK & Irish	Sydney suburbs	431	Rebecca	Kavita,[3] Susie, Gemma, Lisa, Grainne, Diya, Siobhan, Celine, Michelle, Aoife	2015	Yes
German	Sydney suburbs	153	Nicole	Katja, Heike, Stefanie, Annika, Daniela, Petra, Katrin	2012	Yes
Indian	Sydney city	4,800+	Aditi	Archana, Pooja, Sunita, Jyoti, Simran, Kavita	Dec 2015	Yes
Desi (South Asian)[4]	Melbourne city / Melbourne suburbs (2 groups run by same admins)	500 / 1,000+	Priya, Nisha	Usha, Archana	2014	Yes
Brazilian	Melbourne city	1,000+	Kate, Ana	Maria[5]	2011	Yes
Malaysian	Australia	378	Shelly	Sheila, Winnie	2012	Yes
Swedish	Sydney suburbs	94	Eva	Lina	2012	No
German	Melbourne city	300	Tanja	-	2013	No

(Continued)

Table A.1 (Cont.)

Place of origin	Place of residence¹	No. of members (at time of administrator interview)	Administrators interviewed	Members interviewed	Year of group creation	Intentionally women-only?²
Persian	Sydney suburbs	258	Yasmin	-	2014	Yes
Spanish-speaking	Melbourne city	245	Maria	-	2014	No
Swedish	Sydney city	242	Jenni	-	2013	No
Singaporean	Melbourne city	139	Karen	-	2009	Yes
Scandinavian	Melbourne suburbs	21	Sabina	-	2014	No

Notes:

1 'Sydney / Melbourne suburbs' means the group covered a specific sub-metropolitan area of the city. 'Sydney / Melbourne city' means the group covered the whole metropolitan area.

2 This issue is discussed in more detail in Chapter 4.

3 Kavita was a member of both the UK/Irish and Indian mothers' groups.

4 Desi is a term used to refer to South Asian people (most commonly from India, Pakistan, and Bangladesh, but not exclusively). It can be used to refer to a South Asian diasporic identity (Kim, H. (Ed.), *Making Diaspora in a Global City*, Routledge, 2014).

5 Maria was interviewed as the administrator of the Spanish-speaking mothers' group but also discussed her experience of being a member of the Brazilian mothers' group.

Appendix 2

Interview guide

MIGRATION

Tell me about how you came to live in Australia

- When, whence, why, with whom?
- Feelings and expectations; challenges/surprises
- Did you join any online groups or forums before you left?
- Do you think you'll stay in Australia?

MOTHERHOOD

Tell me about becoming a mother for the first time

- Challenges / surprises
- Did you join any online groups or forums specifically relating to becoming a mother beforehand or in the early days?

MOTHERING AWAY FROM HOME

Where is 'home' to you?

What is it like for you, raising your children in a different country?

- Challenges / benefits
- How do you think it would have been different if you were raising your children "back home"?
- Areas of conflict/difference
- What is it like being a [nationality] mum in Australia?

USE OF TECHNOLOGY AND SOCIAL MEDIA

How important are technology and social media to you, in terms of managing being a mother away from home?

- Time spent / frequency of use of online communication tools
- What sort of tools or platforms do you use for this?

[GROUP]

- Do you remember how you first came across the group?
- When did you join (date, and in relation to migration and motherhood timelines)?
- Why? Was it important to you that the group was just for mothers? Just for people from the same/similar background? Local to your area of [city]? Why?
- What did you hope would happen when you joined the group? What were you looking for?
- What were your first impressions of the group?
- Did you post straight away? Read through posts? What did you think about the posts you read?
- About the group now

  a   How would you say the group has changed since you joined?
  b   What sort of topics are discussed in it? Which topics come up most often? Which topics gain the most passionate responses?
  c   Are there particular times of year when there are more posts, or more emotional posts?
  d   Have there been any tensions in the group? Caused by?
  e   Is the group only for mothers? If so, what do you think about that? How would you feel if there were dads in the group? Would you expect the group to be consulted if dads were going to be able to join?
  f   Do you feel like the other group members are your friends? How would you describe them if not?
  g   What do you most like about the group? Anything you don't like? What do you use it for?
  h   Why do you think other people use the group? What do they use it for?
  i   Have you ever posted? Post regularly? Why/ why not?

    - If you have, what sort of things have you posted about?

  j   Do you respond to other people's posts? Why/why not?

    - If you have, what sort of posts do you tend to reply to? Why?

  k   How do you access the group? Laptop/smartphone etc.? How often do you see posts (come up in feed all the time, or check specifically on occasion, only look when want to find info/post)?

- For admins only:

  a When did you become an admin?
  b How do you decide who can join? Do you ever not let anyone join? How do people find out about it?
  c Number of posts (per hour/day), number of responses per post, estimated number of active posters etc.
  d What is your role as administrator of the group? Do you have explicit (written) rules/guidelines? If not, are there implicit rules?
  e How much time do you spend on running the group?

- For members only:

  a Do you know if the group has explicit (written) rules/guidelines? If not, are there implicit rules? Can you think of any kinds of posts or behaviour that would not be allowed?

- Impact in / interaction with offline world?

  a You mentioned X, Y, and Z were challenges you faced – has the group helped you deal with any of these challenges? How?
  b Have you ever made a decision (big or small) based on information or opinions offered by the group? Or have you been influenced by opinions in the group?
  c Have you met up with anyone who you met for the first time in this online group?
  d Do you arrange meet-ups for the group?
  e What difference would you notice in your life if the group disappeared forever overnight?
  f What does your partner/other friends/family think about the group (if at all)?

- How does it feel to be connected to other local [group] mothers through the group?
- How does it feel to have this community of [group] mothers through this group?
- Does it affect how you feel about your local community here in Sydney?
- Does it affect how you feel about your links with home, or the [group] community (here or more broadly in the world)?
- Do you think it has changed your experience of motherhood, (for yourself, how you feel, how you identify OR for how you raise your kids)?

Index

administrators 11, 30, 33–34, 37–39,
77–101, 128; as accidental community
managers 37, 78, 95, 96–98; as leaders
79, 96–98, 128; pride 35, 39, 79, 96,
128; spouses' perspectives 60, 78,
83–84, 95, 97, 99–100; visibility 78, 80,
96–98, 128; *see also* boundary work;
content curation; emotional curation;
meta-maternal practices; online
community managers
affective settlement 16–17, 52, 71, 85,
99–100, 129
Anderson, B. R. O. G 17–18, 29, 44,
105–106, 124

belonging 44, 64–66, 80–81, 86, 88, 100;
through relationships 16, 51–53
boundaries 28; based on gender 81–86,
133–134; based on geography 86–88;
based on motherhood 28–29, 81–84,
87, 93; boundary work 79–86, 89–92,
99, 128
Brazil: migrants from 2–3, 36, 38–39, 68,
88; Brazilian mothers' groups 2, 29,
39, 41–42, 87–88, 92, *134*

citizenship 2, 40; digital citizenship 81,
86, 94
Collins, P. H. 4, 7, 15, 54, 95, 99–100
communities of care see horizontal care
community building 5, 19, 100; as unpaid
labour 80; as gendered settlement
practice 69, 71
community mothering 77–80, 93, 95,
98–100, 110, 112, 128
content curation 93–94
COVID-19 x
cultural transmission 4, 63–64, 100 *see
also* language; mothering for ethnicity

diaspora: and belonging 87–88; diaspora
communities and networks 6, 19, 87,
106–107, 110, 130; diasporic intimacy
67; diasporic maternal identity 108–110,
130; digital diaspora 1, 87
digital community mothering *see*
community mothering
digital labour 77–80, 84–85, 98–99,
128–129; digital housewife 98–99
Diminescu, D. 16, 51–52, 105
disconnection 64–65
domestic labour: paid 5–6, 37, 55, 117;
unpaid 85, 98, 111

emotional affordances 17, 63, 65, 71, 78
emotional curation 91–94; managing
conflict 91–93, 96
emotional labour 19, 61, 91–94, 96,
128–129
emotions: as barrier to belonging 18, 51,
55–61, 64–65, 71; in interviewing
12–14; and migration 16–18, 51–52,
55–58; *see also* disconnection, failure,
friendship, guilt, homesickness
ethnic socialisation *see* mothering for
ethnicity, cultural transmission
extended families 35, 54–56, 60–61, 100,
116–119, 122

Facebook groups: as comfort and
security 64–65, 68–69, 89, 129; history
of 5, 33; for migrant mothers 8, 33–35,
28–29, 80–81, 86–88, 110, 124
133–134, ; for mothers 33–35, 65, 118,
124; naming practices 28–29, 80, 87;
privacy and disclosure 10–11, 30–31,
44, 70, 84–86; as transactional spaces
27, 39, 43, 94
Facebook friends 30, 40, 70, 85–86

failure 52, 61–64, 122–124
family support 35–36, 55–56
feminism: Black feminist thought 18–19, 95, 99–100; matricentric feminism 6–7, 14–15, 127; in digital media scholarship 10, 19, 80, 84–85, 98–99; in migration research 4–5, 19, 71, 80; standpoint theory 6–7, 14
Fisher, K. 28, 37–38, 42
Francisco-Menchavez, V. 4–6, 16, 52, 60, 67, 71
friendship 6, 52, 56–58, 65–71; *see also* relational settlement, isolation

Gedalof, I. 5, 16, 51–52, 63, 69, 105
gender equality 7, 14, 82; as Swedish cultural norm 82, 107, 111–13
gender: and decision-making 9; and guilt 60–61; and information-seeking 83–84; and labour 55–56, 78, 85–86, 98–99, 111, 116; and migration 3–5, 69; and parenting 31, 81–83, 127; and social capital 85; and social media practices 83–85; and sociality 81, 83–84; and trust 85–86
Germany: German maternal practices 113–116; migrants from 2–3, 35–36, 57–58, 107–108; German mothers' groups 29, 62–64, 68, 82, *134; see also* swaddling
guilt 16, 60–61, 110, 118–119

Hage, G. 16, 52, 65
home 54–57, 64–65, 67–68, 115, 122–123
home-building 16, 43, 52, 65, 68–69, 129
homesickness 14, 56, 58–60, 62, 65
horizontal care 6, 16, 52, 60, 71,

imaginaries 17–18, 106, 123–124, 128, 131; migrant maternal imaginaries 17–18, 106–107, 110, 115–116, 129–130
imagined communities 18, 71, 105–107, 123–124 *see also* Anderson, B. R. O. G.
imagined communities of maternal practice 107, 114–119
India: migrants from 2–3, 5, 34, 36–37, 77, 94; Indian mothers' groups 8, 34–35, 40–41, 43, 66–67, *134*
infertility 119–120
information grounds theory 28, 37–38, 42
information: information exchange as settlement activity 39–42; information exchange as social strategy 42–44;

information needs 38–41, 65, 93; *see also* information grounds theory; social information foraging
intersectionality 13–15, 128, 130
interviews 2–3, 8–14; and shared social locations 11–14; as emotional encounters 12–14
intimacy 52–53, 66–71, 129
Ireland: migrants from 2–3, 50, 57; Irish mothers' groups 42, 50 *see also* British and Irish mothers' groups
isolation 4, 51, 53–56, 61, 71, 131 *see also* friendship

Jarrett, K. 19, 80, 95, 98–99

language: as barrier to seeking support 31–32, 53; and identity 28–29, 63, 87, 111, 122; raising bilingual children 27, 63–65, 87, 115; *see also* cultural transmission; mothering for ethnicity
latent ties 67–69
Liamputtong, P. 4, 53, 105, 113

Malaysia: migrants from 2–3, 57, 61–62, 122; Malaysian mothers' groups 40, 42, 89–90, *134*
Manohar, N. N.: good motherhood 4; migrant women's community-building and care 5, 19, 69, 71, 100; social capital 86; social locations in qualitative research 12–14; *see also* mothering for ethnicity
mapping exercise 8–9, 13–14, 29–30
maternal mental health 4, 40, 53, 56, 59, 131
maternal narratives 107, 110, 114–115, 119, 121, 123–124, 129–130
maternal practices 4, 7, 32, 91–94, 99, 107–108, 113–117, 121; *see also* imagined communities of maternal practice; swaddling; motherhood
matrescence 9, 129
memory 106–110, 121–123, 128
meta-maternal practices 18–19, 80, 93–95, 99–100, 128
migration: as emotional experience 16–18, 51–52, 55–58; as disruption 52, 64–65, 107, 115, 121–124, 129; family migration 2, 6; lifestyle migration 9, 11; love migration 9, 11; managed migration 3; middling migration 3, 11; temporary migration 2–3, ; skilled migration 3

mobility 16, 51–52, 58, 86, 88
motherhood: combative mothering
    91–93; compassionate mothering
    91–93, 98, 128; good motherhood 4,
    18, 92, 105, 110–111, 117, 121–122;
    motherhood studies 4, 7; motherwork
    7; as belonging to private sphere 7, 54,
    93, 97–98; as socially constructed 4,
    14–15, 38; new motherhood 33–34, 65,
    81–82, 112, 131; *see also* maternal
    practices; matrescence, mothering for
    ethnicity
mothering for ethnicity 105, 110–111,
    63 *see also* cultural transmission;
    language
mothers' groups 31–34, 50–51, 53, 82,
    104; *see also* Facebook groups for
    mothers; online mothers' groups

national identity 105–106, 110–111, 119

O'Reilly, A. 4, 7, 71
offline meet-ups 11, 39–40, 66–68, 87, 95
online community management 19, 78–
    80, 91, 98–99; as community service
    19, 88, 100, 104, 128; as feminised
    profession 78, 98; parenting metaphors
    77, 79, 99; power 79–80, 96; *see also*
    administrators; meta-maternal
    practices
online community managers *see*
    administrators
online mothers' groups 32–33, 118, 120

parents' groups *see* mothers' groups
Persian mothers' groups 34, 39, 81, *134*;
    migrants from Iran 2, 36
playgroups 31–32, 51, 53–54, 63–64, 68, 95
positionality 11–14

relational settlement 16, 41, 51–52, 56,
    65–71, 84, 129
relational sociology 15–16

relationality 15–16, 128
research ethics 10–11
research methods 8–10; see also survey;
    interviews; mapping exercise

settlement 16–19, 31–34, 38–41, 43, 71,
    88, 128; see also affective settlement;
    home-building; relational settlement
Singapore: migrants from Singapore 3,
    55; Singaporean mothers' groups
    40–41, 94, 96, *134*; participants'
    experiences as migrants in Singapore
    42, 117–118
social information foraging 28, 42, 84
sociality 42–43, 66–71, 84–85; casual
    intimacy 66–67; intermediate ties
    67–69; social infrastructure 56, 59,
    66, 70–71, 100, 110, 129; *see also*
    friendship
solidarity 6–7, 62–65, 105, 110
survey 8–10, 43–44
swaddling 107, 113–116, 124
Sweden: migrants from 2–3, 27, 63, 122;
    Swedish mothers' groups 28, 40, 81,
    111–113, *134; see also* gender equality

transnational caregiving 1, 4–5, 60–61,
    84–85
transnational mothering 2, 4–5, 105
transnational ties 88, 130
trust 62, 89–92; distrust 32, 89–90; and
    gender 84–86; generalised trust 87;
    trusted information 32; and sameness
    80, 87, 89–91; *see also* boundaries

United Kingdom: migrants from 2–3, 13,
    108, 122; British and Irish mothers'
    groups 12, 29, 60, 67, 110, *134*

WhatsApp 6, 10, 36, 83, 85, 104
work: as identity 55; as opportunity for
    social interaction 55, 66; workplaces
    38, 55, 97, 128

Lightning Source UK Ltd.
Milton Keynes UK
UKHW030704090222
398410UK00004B/38